Printed in the USA
CPSIA information can be obtained
at www.ICGtesting.com
LVHW012237240823
756179LV00005B/111

WANTED: Christian Educators with Character

James R. Virtue, EdD

Faithful Life Publishers
North Fort Myers, FL

FaithfulLifePublishers.com

Wanted: Christian Educators with Character

© 2015 James R. Virtue, EdD
ISBN: 978-1-63073-102-1

Published and printed by:
Faithful Life Publishers • North Fort Myers, FL 33903
888.720.0950 • info@FaithfulLifePublishers.com
www.FaithfulLifePublishers.com

Scripture is taken from the New King James Version.

Printed in the United States of America
19   18   17   16   15   1 2 3 4 5

PREFACE

Education has seen many changes over the last several years and it has become difficult to keep up with what is expected. As the various changes have been proposed, we have seen new standards adopted every few years and this requires a shift in the educational strategies in order to meet the expected standards. Many times it seems that we have forgotten that education is for the students and instead we only focus on the standards or on passing "the test."

Many have said, "If we continue to do what we have always done, how can we expect to see any improvement." On the other hand, we have those who have a desire to get back to the basics of teaching reading, writing, and arithmetic so our students have a solid foundation for the future. They don't think schools should be involved in the social issues of the day. This has caused a dilemma in our schools across the country. It has become frustrating for many teachers in their effort to meet the needs of the students while they are expected to teach to the test.

I have been involved in various aspects of education for the past 40 years and have seen the importance of having qualified teachers in the classroom. I believe one of the greatest needs for teachers is in the area of their character. If we have solid character, it helps us to deal with the many issues we face in the classroom. I believe that Christian educators, whether we are in a Christian school or a secular school, need to establish the character by which we will live and work. This will help us to be more effective in ministering to our students.

WANTED: Christian Educators with Character

Our society is rapidly changing toward an anti-Christian attitude in many areas, making it important for us to establish where we stand in regard to the Truth of God's Word. If we don't stand firm, we will begin to slide away from the Truth and lose our spiritual impact upon our students and their families.

Over the years I have seen many families come to trust Christ as their Savior because they enrolled their children in a Christian school and because of the example and witness of Christian educators with character. I have seen this impact on the families decline over the years and believe that we need to examine ourselves as Christian educators in regard to our testimony to others. I have also seen students and families begin to attend a church because of the example set by a teacher in a secular school. We can all have an impact.

Secular education has gone further and further away from anything that might resemble Christianity and I believe there is a real need for solid Christian teachers in this system to stand for the Truth in these schools. I believe that Christian teachers can make a difference.

I trust that as you read this book you will be challenged to examine yourself in light of God's Word to determine if you are living the life of character that will enable you to be the testimony you need to be in your personal life and your professional life.

TABLE OF CONTENTS

Chapter 1

Introduction

Throughout Scripture there are many references to the character and the daily living expectations for a believer. Two passages that are used primarily for leaders in a church are found in Paul's letters of First Timothy and Titus. However, the twenty characteristics found in these passages, as well as others, are applied to all Christians in Paul's other letters. As we consider Christian educators with character, we will look at several passages that will summarize for us the character we should find exhibited in all Christians, but primarily, for the purposes of this book, in Christian educators.

The focus of this book is on Christian educators in general, not just Christian educators in Christian schools. However, because of my experience in working in a Christian school setting, my thoughts will probably lean toward those educators in Christian schools, although I will attempt to show application to all Christian educators.

If someone asked you to describe what a Christian educator looks like, how would you describe them? We know that the image of an educator means different things to different people. A young student may visualize an educator as one who cares about them and cares about what they do; a teenager may visualize their educator as one who is "too strict" (or "too lenient") or gives them too much homework; a parent may visualize an educator as one who is not easy to communicate with or who takes things out on their child; and the list could go on and on. There are so many perceptions about educators that many times we lose our focus of what an educator really is, or should be. I'm sure you have heard it said that "perception is reality." Therefore, it is important that Christian educators clearly demonstrate the reality of a Christian life to avoid wrong perceptions.

Most of us have our own image of an educator in general and that image becomes more specific when we think about a Christian educator. The image varies depending upon who we are, what we do, and who we associate with on a regular basis. A purpose of this book is to help us understand who and what a Christian educator should be, based on Biblical principles. Christian educators should always be concentrated on what God wants us to be and how He wants us to use our talents and giftedness in the ministry to which He has called us, whether it be in a Christian school or a secular school.

In his foreword to Dr. Lowrie's book, *To Those Who Teach in Christian Schools*, Gene Garrick speaks of the difference between a Christian educator and an educator who is a Christian. An educator who is a Christian does not necessarily understand a Biblical worldview nor how to integrate Scripture into each subject they teach. On the other hand, a Christian educator "assures that all the teaching, activities, and relationships are in alignment with his Christian view of life and with the teaching of the Scripture" (p. i). This is the purpose of this book – to challenge every educator who is a Christian to become a better Christian educator.

As you, no doubt, have experienced, character is a quality that is lacking in our society today. Unfortunately, this lack of character has spilled over into the lives of Christians in general, and for our topic of discussion, Christian educators specifically. As Christian educators, we must determine in our hearts and minds that we are going to model proper character to our students. If we model proper character, along with our teaching of proper character, we will be able to have maximum impact on our students. We would all probably agree that if what we do (how we live) doesn't match up with what we say, we will not have much impact on those we teach.

Unfortunately, there are many times in our lives that we allow our character to slip a notch. We sometimes do this by deviating from an accepted standard, and when we slip once, it is easier to slip again. The questions we must answer are: "What causes us to slip?" "How do we stop slipping?" "What happens to our influence during the slipping?" and "How can we recover from slipping?"

It is important that I clarify that I do not believe every standard that a school has is Biblical in nature. Many of them are simply standards which are designed to allow the organization to run in a more effective and efficient manner. However, whether a teacher lives by these standards and/or enforces these standards becomes an aspect of our character, even if the standard has no relationship to the Bible.

There can be a number of things that would influence a Christian educator to deviate from the accepted norms established by their administration, which is one of the major areas of "slipping." One factor may be a friendship established with a parent that influences how we treat their student. Another factor could be the influence, or the wealth, or the status of a parent which causes us to be more lenient with their student for fear we might cause them to withdraw (and the school needs the money!). Another factor could be the sweet, innocent looks of a "cute" student. Or, it could be, we don't agree with the established standards so we cut corners with some of them. In all of these areas, and more, it is important for each of us to examine our hearts to determine what we need to correct in our lives as well as in our practices.

One year when I was the Headmaster of a Christian school, I also taught a class the period before lunch. After a number of weeks, when the students had adjusted to the fact that the Headmaster was their teacher, they tried to convince me to dismiss them early for lunch. My response was that the school policy stated that no class was to be dismissed for lunch until the bell rang. Their response was typical, "But you are in charge of the policy. No one will question you." They were saying, in a sense, that breaking the rule is okay if you don't get in trouble for it. I had a decision to make – maintain my integrity and enforce the policy, or let them go early and make them wonder what other policies I might be willing to break. If I let them go early I also would have to deal with the example I was setting for the other teachers. This may seem like such a small issue, but it can be the setting of a pattern for breaking other rules since I can get away with it.

Teachers are faced with these types of decisions every day. We know what the policy states, but it is tempting to "give in" to make the student(s) happy (for the moment), or to avoid a confrontation with a parent, or some other perceived pleasure. After all, if we don't get caught, is it wrong? I have heard many teachers say, "It's easier to ask for forgiveness than for permission." However, we must determine what our character is, and then we must stand firm for doing what is right. Dr. Bob Jones often said, "It is never right to do wrong in order to get a chance to do right." You are all familiar with the question "What Would Jesus Do?" This can be used as a good reference point in our desire to live a life of character.

The Scriptures are full of examples of people who did not follow the standard that was established, and as a result, they had to pay the consequences – some sooner, some later. A vivid illustration is the behavior of Uzzah in 2 Samuel 6. The Israelites were bringing the Ark of the Covenant back to Jerusalem. God had established very strict guidelines as to how the ark was to be moved (men were to carry it on the appropriate poles) and no one was to touch it. The Israelites were moving it in a wrong fashion (they put it on a cart which was being pulled by oxen). This caused the ark to tip as the oxen stumbled, as if it were going to fall over. Uzzah did what he thought was right by reaching up to keep it from falling over. As a result of touching the ark, he was immediately struck dead. What a vivid lesson on obedience – regardless of the fact that he thought it was the correct thing to do! Have we ever done something that we "thought" was right even though we had been instructed as to the proper way of doing it? Have we been enticed to bend the rules just a little bit because it was "convenient?" How does our character match up with God's standards?

Chapter 2

THE ESSENCE OF CHARACTER

Character has been defined in a number of ways, but the essence of character is what you do and who you are in all circumstances. Bill Hybels (1987) says that character is "what we do when no one is looking." We know many people who change their behavior as the occasion warrants it demonstrating a lack of character. They try to become all things to all people and they end up not being liked or accepted or trusted by anyone. People of character are willing to stand up for what they believe, regardless of the circumstances and/or the opinions of others, and people of character will take this stand without being obnoxious about it. Our character should reflect the character of Christ.

Stephen Covey (1989) has said that character grows "in the soil of experience with the fertilization of example, the moisture of ambition, and the sunshine of satisfaction. Character cannot be purchased, bargained for, inherited, rented, or imported from afar. It must be home-grown" (p. 273).

The root meaning of the word "character" refers to something cut or engraved into an object that marks it unmistakably for what it is. For example, many people wear jewelry that has their name engraved on it. There is no mistake as to whom it belongs if there is a question raised, because of the engraving. Character persists day after day, regardless of the circumstances. It is not a collection of behaviors or intentions, but a matter of the heart. Our character is engraved on our hearts which means it will not change. What does change is how our living matches up with that inward character.

Since the word "Christian" means "like Christ," it is logical that we should discuss how we live out our definition of being a Christian. However, it is certainly much easier to discuss being Christ-like than actually living Christ-like in our daily lives. What is involved in being Christ-like? I believe the best way to understand the meaning of being like Christ is to look at some people in the Bible who were considered to be Christ-like.

One of the first people to come to my mind would be David. He is referred to as a man after God's own heart (1 Samuel 13:14). We quickly recognize that David was not a perfect man and yet we would consider him as "Christ-like." Probably the most important reason for this is that when he was confronted with his sin, he repented and made every effort to rectify it. He didn't live his life making excuses for his failures, although he did have to live his life paying the consequences for his failures. When you fail, do you have a tendency to make excuses for your failures or do you repent when confronted?

For example, if you were to break one of the rules established for you as a teacher and the administrator calls you into his/her office, what is your response? Do you admit it and accept the consequences, or do you make up an excuse for why it happened? We must be willing to admit our mistakes.

Another person who comes to mind is Joseph. Joseph was mistreated by his brothers and sold into slavery. He fled from the temptation of his master's wife, and yet he was put into prison based on false accusations. In everything we read about Joseph, he was forgiving and did not hold grudges. He was faithful to God and allowed God to use him where he was and in the circumstances in which he found himself. When you are in difficult circumstances, do you forgive or do you hold grudges? For example, if a parent gets upset with you and calls you names and threatens you, do you forgive them, or do you take out your frustrations on their student?

Paul is another person of integrity. Prior to his conversion, Paul was a zealous persecutor of the Christians because he believed God wanted him to protect Judaism. After his salvation, he had the same zeal in preaching the Gospel. He suffered many wrongful things done to him, including being stoned and left for dead as well as spending much time in prison, yet he was faithful in his service to the Lord. Are you faithful in serving God, even when people "persecute" you when you have done nothing wrong? We know that any "persecution" we may face is minimal in comparison to what others may face. However, we must remain strong even with things such as people, or students, mocking us when we have done nothing wrong.

As I stated earlier, the basic character of Christian educators is applicable to all Christians, although Christian educators find themselves in a number of different relationships in relation to the character expected. Christian educators relate to their administrators, other educators, students, parents, the community, the church, the board (if the school has a board), and the pastor (if it is a church related school). What kind of relationships are we building with those we come into contact on a daily basis and are those relationships in agreement with Christian character? What kind of character do we display when our administrator asks us to do something? How do we respond when we are asked to do something that is unethical? Are we honest with our students and their parents?

When I was a young teacher, I caught one of my students cheating on a test. He denied it but I was able to produce evidence to prove it and then he admitted it. His immediate reaction, after admitting it, was asking me not to contact his parents. He made all kinds of promises to me that he would keep if I wouldn't call his parents. I had a choice to make. Would I be honest with his parents in regard to the work he was doing or would I let it slide and try to work with him? I chose to contact his parents and because of that phone call, built a good relationship with his parents, and the student, which lasted for many years.

Most teachers have heard students requesting that they not teach today, just give us a "play day." Along with that request comes the statement, "All the other teacher do this." From an ethical perspective, what are we going to do? We are there to provide an education and not give "play days."

The challenge I would give comes from an often quoted adage, "What you do speaks so loud I can't hear what you're saying." We owe it to our constituents, as well as to God, to be examples of character as well as educators of character. We need to "practice what we preach."

Crucified with Christ ~ Galatians 2:20

All Christians must begin their focus with the principle of being crucified with Christ (*I have been crucified with Christ; it is no longer I who live, but Christ lives in me; and the life which I now live in the flesh I live by faith in the Son of God, who loved me and gave Himself for me.* Galatians 2:20). We understand that God doesn't want us physically dead, but He wants us to be dead to self. This means that in our day-to-day lives we focus on God and what He wants us to do instead of focusing on ourselves and what we want to do.

WANTED: Christian Educators with Character

In 1 Corinthians 10:31, Paul writes *Therefore, whether you eat or drink, or whatever you do, do all to the glory of God.* In the context of this passage, he is defining for the Corinthian believers how they must be careful of how they live because of the impact they might have on the "weaker" Christians. His point is that if we cause the weaker brother to stumble, we are not bringing glory to God. Ultimately, our entire focus is to be on how Christ wants us to live. We are to be Christ-like examples for others.

Some educators become territorial in their school, and their ministry within the school, and become concerned only with "their" part of the school instead of the school as a whole. They do this because they have not died to self. Any educator who makes a comment to the effect that "I'm not going to do that because..." has basically said, "I'm not crucified with Christ, I'm going to do what I think is best for me." Please understand that I don't expect anyone to follow blindly and do every little thing they are asked to do without raising legitimate questions. It's the attitude that is at issue.

There is nothing wrong with an educator wanting the best for their area of the school, but the focus has to be on what is the best for the entire school – what is the "big" picture. Sometimes it is necessary to sacrifice in one area to make the overall school function more effectively. Many times this is an issue in a church-related school where facilities are shared by the church and school. A big question in this circumstance is who gets priority in each area and who is responsible for each area. An educator who has "crucified" self will not have a problem in sacrificing when asked to do so for the betterment of the overall ministry/school. I will hasten to add that there is only so much sacrificing that a school can expect from an educator when it comes to issues like budget and salary needs. Administrators need to make sure their teachers are taken care of.

In some schools there seems to be a competition as to which teacher is better, or which teacher is liked better, or which teacher works harder. It has been said that much more can be accomplished when no one cares who gets the credit. Christian educators should not be concerned as to who is better, or who is liked better – our concern should be on whether God is pleased and whether He is receiving the glory. Remember, we are crucified (dead) and He is living through us. Therefore, our focus should be on Him.

Fruit of the Spirit ~ Galatians 5:22-24

Galatians 5:22-24 says, *But the fruit of the Spirit is love, joy, peace, longsuffering, kindness, goodness, faithfulness, gentleness, self-control. Against such there is no law.*

The verses prior to these (vv. 19-21) have an emphasis on the works of the flesh so it is obvious that Paul is making a contrast between the works of the flesh and the fruit of the Spirit. A machine in a factory can work and manufacture a product, but it can never produce fruit because fruit must grow out of life. In this case, Paul is saying that the fruit comes from the believer because of the life of the Spirit within the believer. Stuart Briscoe (1993) says that "the aspects of the fruit of the Spirit listed by Paul could just as easily be listed as the characteristics of the nature of God" (p. 6). As we live under the control of the Spirit, we will exhibit the nature of God!

When we think of works, we typically think about effort and work, but when we think of fruit, we typically think about beauty and something that is good (something we enjoy). We also must consider that fruit has seed(s) through which it produces more fruit. Therefore, as we consider this passage, we must remember that each of the fruit mentioned produces more of that fruit; i.e. love produces more love; joy produces more joy; etc.

Paul lists the fruit of love first because all of the other fruit really grow out of love. When we think of love as a Christian, we usually think of 1 Corinthians 13 – the great love chapter in the Bible. There is a comparison between the fruit of the Spirit in Galatians 5:22-23 and the eight characteristics of love in 1 Corinthians 13:4-8.

When we live in love, we will experience joy which is described as an inward peace and sufficiency that is not affected by outward circumstances. When we combine love and joy, we will have peace – the peace of God (*and the peace of God, which surpasses all understanding, will guard your hearts and minds through Christ Jesus.* Philippians 4:7). These first three qualities – love, joy, and peace – express the Godward aspect of the Christian life.

When we look at the next three qualities – long-suffering, gentleness, and goodness – we see the man-ward aspect of the Christian life. Long-suffering speaks of endurance without quitting and typically speaks of our relationship to people, not with things. Long-suffering has the idea of taking a long time to reach our boiling point as we deal with people. It also has the idea of refusing to seek revenge. All Christian educators need to consider this quality as we think about how we deal with all of those we come into contact with in the school setting – students, parents, colleagues, administrators, etc. Are we long-suffering, or do we tend to explode too quickly? If we have a student that irritates us or is obnoxious, how do we react? Are we long-suffering, or do we "let him/her have it?"

Kindness is another word for gentleness and deals very specifically with how we treat others. Someone has said that acting kindly toward others out of a heart of love is like having the hide of a rhinoceros but the heart of a mother. To act kindly is to be useful to the other person by meeting a need in their life. It's interesting to note that we can't act kindly out of our own ability, but only as we allow the grace of God to flow over into our relationships with others. Goodness describes our love in action and complements the idea of kindness. We do "good" when we sow goodness on those we teach and those we work with.

The final three qualities of the fruit of the Spirit are directed toward us. Faithfulness is dependability and causes us to consider if we are dependable to do our best each day in our teaching and in sharing Christ with our students. Gentleness is the right use of power and authority. A synonym of gentleness is meekness which has the idea of being strong, but having that strength under control. When a wild stallion is broken so it can be ridden, it still has its strength but that strength is now under the control of the rider. As a Christian educator, we must be careful of how we use our power and authority and determine to only use it to bring glory to God, not to get what we want and bring glory to ourselves. Our strength doesn't leave us but it is to be under the control of God, not ourselves. Self-control has a similar thought because we must learn to control ourselves through the power of Christ. As a Christian educator, it is important to exhibit self-control toward the students we teach so they are able to learn from our example.

We know that fruit doesn't just grow without the right conditions. Paul discusses these conditions in relation to the fruit of the Spirit in the Galatians passage as well. We should understand that the flesh (the sin nature) cannot produce the fruit of the Spirit; only the Spirit can do that. We are able to tell the difference because when the Spirit produces the fruit, God gets the glory and the Christian does not even recognize his/her level of involvement. However, when the flesh produces the fruit, the Christian is inwardly proud of himself/herself and becomes "puffed up" when others compliment him.

Fruit must be cultivated and in Galatians 5:25-26, Paul tells us that just as fruit cannot grow in every climate, the fruit of the Spirit cannot grow in every person's life. The fruit of the Spirit only grows where there is an abundance of the Spirit and the Word. Paul tells us to "walk in the Spirit" which means that we are not to get ahead of the Spirit, nor are we to fall behind the Spirit. To cultivate the fruit, we must regularly practice the spiritual disciplines of studying the Word, praying, worshiping and praising God, and fellowshipping with God's people. Cultivation also involves pulling the weeds (getting rid of things in our lives that hinder us) so the seed can take root and can grow unencumbered to produce the fruit. Do we have any weeds in our life that need to be pulled?

It is interesting to note that fruit is produced to be eaten, not to sit on a shelf someplace. Consider the number of people around us who are hungry for love, joy, peace, etc. Our students and their parents will sense that we have something they lack when they see us exhibiting the fruit. This will draw them to us so we are able to share our faith with them. After all, we produce fruit, not for our own consumption, but for the purpose of feeding and helping others.

Character of the Beattitudes ~ Matthew 5:1-12

Another passage of Scripture to help us understand how a Christian educator is to live a life of character is the beginning of the Sermon on the Mount in Matthew 5. According to Lloyd-Jones (1976), the Beattitudes provide for us a description of the character of a Christian. This is followed by how our character is proven because of the reaction of the world to our character; then the remainder of the Sermon provides particular examples and illustrations of how a person with this character lives in the world. We cannot live the life unless we first develop the character.

WANTED: Christian Educators with Character

Swindoll (1981) states that the Beattitudes provide a "Portrait of a Servant." He emphasizes that a Christian does not have the option of picking and choosing which of the character traits he wishes to have, but must incorporate all of them into his life. When we consider this in relationship to being a Christian educator, we very easily realize that an educator is to be a servant to the students he teaches and to their parents. This does not mean that we do everything they want us to do, but it has the idea of meeting their needs by providing the education the student deserves. If we don't have the proper characteristics of a servant, we won't serve, and if we don't serve, we will not have an effective ministry.

Most Christians have a difficult time living according to the standards set in the Sermon because they haven't developed the right "Christian" thinking. When a person accepts Christ as their Savior and becomes a Christian, their thinking must undergo a paradigm shift to think like Christ (Philippians 2:5) and to then be able to live in dependence upon Him. When we realize we can't live the Christian life unless we think like a Christian, we have taken the first step of changing our thinking.

The Beattitudes focus on happiness. Everyone wants to be happy; people search everywhere for happiness. As Christians, we know how to be happy – live according to the Beattitudes which, of course, is easier said than done. However, I trust as you read this section, you will begin to clarify your thinking and begin to develop (or continue to build on) the character described, which will result in right thinking, right living, and effective ministry.

The first Beattitude states, *"Blessed are the poor in spirit..."* This concept is essential because it speaks of an emptying of self and we know there must be an emptying before there can be a filling. No one can enter the kingdom without being "poor in spirit." The perspective is that we realize we are nothing in ourselves. Sometimes educators get the idea that because of their degree(s) or because of their experience, they have an advantage over other educators. Jesus says that we are not to think as the world thinks, depending on self-reliance and self-confidence. Being poor in spirit means a complete absence of pride (that's convicting even to think about!). It means taking on the attitude of Jesus who was equal with God, but didn't worry about His reputation and took upon Himself the form of a servant (Philippians 2:5-11). As Christian educators, we must realize that we are called to serve our students (meeting their needs), not to be masters over our students. We must realize that to be the most effective in ministering to our students and their families we can do nothing in and of ourselves, but only what we allow God to do through us. It's not easy to live this way at times because of some of the issues we face. For example, we have an irritating student or we have a parent that questions everything we do as a teacher. Another situation is when a teacher has an administrator who has been out of the classroom for so long they have forgotten what it is like to teach a room full of students on a daily basis. We must remember that we are there to serve and allow God to work through us.

The second Beattitude states *"Blessed are they that mourn..."* In our typical thinking (because we tend to think like the world thinks) we don't like the concept of mourning because it isn't pleasant. When we think of mourning in order to be happy, it doesn't sound logical unless we are thinking like Christ thinks. In this context, we are mourning over the fact of our sins as well as the sins of others. A person who thinks like this is so concerned about the state of our society that they mourn over it. As an educator, do you mourn over your own life and the fact that you are not the example you should be to your students? Do you mourn over the sinful condition of your students and their families? We sometimes express concern over some of the things they do, but we don't really mourn over them. We are content to continue our life and allow them to continue their lifestyle without much more than an occasional passing comment. A mourning Christian is happy when mourning leads to repentance – a change of mind – which leads to a change of lifestyle.

As I have thought about mourning over the sins of others my mind goes back to the occasions I have been involved in major discipline issues in the school. There were a number of times when issues had to be dealt with and decisions had to be made in regard to the consequences handed down to the students. I remember a time when several students had to be expelled and that decision eliminated much of the basketball team. I remember another time when the decision was made to not allow several seniors to march at graduation. I know I suffered in those decisions but I wonder if I really mourned. Was my suffering caused by what I was going through or was it because I was really mourning over the sinful condition of the students. What a serious question this Beattitude raises!

The third Beattitude is *"Blessed are the meek..."* This is drastically opposite of the thinking of the world because their thinking always deals with conquest and they think the winner is always the strongest. The world's concept of being meek is to be timid and afraid. However, a great definition of being meek (as we mentioned previously) is "strength under control." Meekness is an inward view of ourselves, not just an outward demonstration, but an inward spirit. The meek person does not claim to have any rights and does not make any demands for his position, his privileges, his possessions, or his status. A meek man will marvel at how well God and man treat him because he realizes that he doesn't deserve anything.

Have you ever used the expression, "I have my rights!" or, have you ever had a student use that statement on you? It expresses a self-centeredness and un-Biblical view of who we are. I know that teachers in the secular schools operate under a different set of regulations than in Christian schools, primarily because of union contracts. However, even under that scenario, we must be careful that we don't neglect what God has called us to do by focusing on our rights. If we are crucified with Christ (Galatians 2:20) we have given up our rights.

I do understand also that some school administrators may try to take advantage of teachers in an effort to complete a task, to cover a class, or any number of things. I do not believe this is Biblical either as a person needs to be compensated for the time they spend outside of the normal responsibilities.

The fourth Beattitude is *"Blessed are those who hunger and thirst after righteousness..."* We all have a limited understanding of what it means to be hungry and/or thirsty, even though very few of us have been in a situation of starving. When we are hungry or thirsty, we make every effort to find something that will fulfill the need we sense. This Beattitude speaks of those who are hungry and thirsty for righteousness which is another totally foreign concept to a worldly thinking mind. Do you crave righteousness so much that you will go to great lengths to satisfy that craving? Imagine going to church where the entire congregation was hungering and thirsting for righteousness. Do you think anyone would be watching the clock to see when the pastor was going to finish?

As an educator, picture what your classroom would be like if all of your students had a hunger and a thirst for righteousness. We would have so much time to teach our academic subject we wouldn't know how to act. Better yet, picture what your classroom would be like if the teacher (that's you!) hungered and thirsted for righteousness! With this perspective, we would totally change our approach to our students and our teaching. We would be so focused on God and would allow the Holy Spirit to direct our thoughts and actions in such a way that students, and others, would be drawn to Christ through us. We would make sure that our curriculum was Christ-centered and we would incorporate Biblical principles in everything we do. May we be challenged to develop this in our lives and encourage those around us to also develop this mind set.

The fifth Beattitude is *"Blessed are the merciful..."* Aren't you thankful that God has shown you mercy, not only to provide you with salvation, but to show mercy to you on a daily basis? A merciful educator is one who has compassion for a student (or another educator, or a parent) because of their misery and is willing to do what they can to relieve that misery. Many times we feel that we should do something to help a person out, but we never get around to doing anything. Other than Christ, probably the best example of a merciful person in Scripture is the Good Samaritan (Luke 10:30-37). He had compassion on the man who had been beaten and robbed and he actually did something about it – he went to him and took care of him.

As Christian educators we face many kinds of students from year to year with different needs and their families have additional needs. How much mercy do we show them? We feel sorry for some of them, but do we actually do anything to help them relieve the misery they have? How do we minister to a student whose father just lost their job? How do we minister to a student who has lost a close relative to death? How do we minister to a student whose parents' fight all the time when they are home? Do we display mercy?

I received a letter from an alumna of our school about 20 years after she had graduated. In her letter she was thanking the school for ministering to her while she was a student. Her comment was that it was the only place she had peace and experienced stability. She never knew what she would find at home when she arrived there. At the time, I did not realize the need she had in this area. It causes me to wonder whether I would have shown mercy to her and her family if I had known or if I would have just treated the surface needs.

We had another student in our school one year that was a good student and was involved in athletics and other activities. However, I found out that he lived with his step-dad and his new wife. This meant the student was not living with either of his biological parents. His needs were different than those of other students.

Before we move to the next Beattitude, I think it's important for us to again consider the importance of understanding the "big picture" of the Beattitudes and how they relate to the rest of the Sermon on the Mount (Matthew 5-7). The Beattitudes were spoken by Jesus to prepare the people (and us) and His disciples in particular for the remainder of the Sermon. Jesus knew that we could not do what He was going to tell us in the Sermon until we had the appropriate character as defined in the Beattitudes.

When you read the Sermon, some of the things Jesus instructed us to do don't seem logical. Because they don't seem logical, we pass by them with a weak excuse to the effect that those statements must have been meant for people of that day and don't apply to Christians today. However, if we spent our time developing the character of the Beattitudes, we would quickly understand, and would be able to practice, the remainder of the Sermon. It all depends upon our developing the character traits discussed.

Lloyd-Jones (1976) even discusses the importance of the order of the Beattitudes. He states that the first three are concerned with our need and our becoming conscious of our need. Once we are aware of our need, we then hunger and thirst for righteousness which leads to our being filled. Once we are filled with righteousness we have no problem being merciful, being pure in heart, and being peacemakers. Then we come to the result of having this character, which is being persecuted for being righteous because sinners don't like being around someone who is righteous.

The sixth Beattitude is *"Blessed are the pure in heart..."* Those who are pure in heart are those who have mourned over the impurity in their heart and have allowed God to do what is necessary to cleanse it and make it pure. Wouldn't we love to have a teacher who was pure in heart? Wouldn't we love to have a teacher for our students who was pure in heart? Imagine how we would act differently if we had allowed God to cleanse all impurity from our heart. As Christian educators, one of our responsibilities is to be an example for our students. What a great example an educator with a pure heart would be! May I challenge us to mourn over our impure hearts and allow God to cleanse the impurity He uncovers. This is definitely not an easy process because most of us have a lot of impurities that need to be cleansed.

The seventh Beattitude is *"Blessed are the peacemakers..."* When most people think about peace, they think it means there is absence of conflict. However, God sees peace as the presence of righteousness that causes right relationships. Peace comes when the truth is known, the issue is settled, and the parties embrace each other. Many Christian educators feel that peace with other adults can be maintained by avoiding conflict. However, we are not doing God's will if we don't confront sin and restore relationships. Of course, as we deal with student conflict, we must learn to deal with this in a different way as we are training our students to become peacemakers. We have to help them build righteousness into their lives. We cannot simply deal with the issue at hand from a surface perspective but we must get to the root of the issue and begin the discipling process. We must remember that our goal in discipline is to bring our students to a closer relationship with God.

It is interesting to note that later in the Sermon (Matthew 5:39) Jesus instructs us to turn the other cheek if we are wronged and struck on the cheek. In Jewish thought, the "cheek" was the symbol of a relationship; kissing someone's cheek was a sign of peace and fellowship. "Striking someone's cheek" meant that you were attacking the relationship. Turning your other cheek to them was a step of offering to restore the relationship with them. I recognize that kissing someone's cheek is not a common practice in many parts of the United States (in South Florida this is very common); however, I believe it is a great illustration showing the importance of restoring and maintaining close relationships. We become peacemakers when we turn our other check to restore a relationship.

The last Beattitude is *"Blessed are they which are persecuted..."* As stated above, those who live according to the first seven Beattitudes will experience the last one because the life that lives these character traits is so foreign to our evil world that they must react to it. Many also believe that the amount of persecution we will face will be determined by the degree to which we live the first seven Beattitudes. I understand that this is not presenting a very positive incentive for developing this character in our lives. However, when we recognize that God is pleased as we develop this character and we recognize our positive growing relationship with God, we will have all the incentive we need.

As we bring this section to a close, it's almost overwhelming to consider how God expects us to live as Christians and we know that He expects Christian educators to meet the standard, and rise above how the average Christian meets the standard, because we are influencing those who are being taught under our care along with their families. I would suggest that each of us take some time to examine our personal lives and our relationship with Christ to insure that we are living a Christ-like life.

A Mature Christian ~ 1 Timothy 3:1-7; Titus 1:5-10

When we come to the passages in Timothy and Titus, we typically think about pastors and deacons (elders) and their qualifications. However, I believe the qualities listed in these passages can be applied to all Christians and these qualities challenge all of us to be mature Christians. These passages provide for us a profile for testing the maturity level of a Christian. As you know, it takes time to mature and maturity comes as we build our relationship with Christ. Lest you become concerned, I will not deal extensively with each of these 20 qualities, but will choose some that have not been covered in the previous passages and that I believe are more pertinent to Christian educators.

A quality that seems to summarize the rest of the qualities is "above reproach." This can be interpreted in a number of ways but it's also self-descriptive. God wants us to have a good reputation among those both inside our schools and outside of our schools. There is a similarity of this quality to the trait of being "pure in heart" from the Beattitudes. It is challenging for us, both as Christians and as educators, to live a life above reproach. We face many situations on a daily basis in dealing with our students, their parents, our administrators, and our colleagues during which we must be careful to be "above reproach." For example, if you have a meeting with an upset parent, how do you respond? Do you maintain your composure and speak calmly? If you realize you did something wrong, are you willing to admit it and apologize for it? We must be careful in all of our relationships as it takes a lifetime to build a reputation but it can be lost in an instant. I know a man who was a leader in an organization and he was leading a meeting that was dealing with some difficult issues. When a question was asked which put him on the spot, he reacted negatively and yelled at the questioner and everyone else in the meeting. Because of that one negative reaction he was forced to resign his position. Let's determine, with God's help, that we will build our reputation, not react negatively, and be above reproach.

The next quality we will consider is "respectable." This means that we live a well-ordered life or that we are well-behaved. We are to live our lives in a way that our lives show the teachings of the Word of God. Part of the way we demonstrate this is that we obey those in authority over us and are not argumentative. This does not mean that we have to always agree, but it means that if we disagree, we do it with a godly attitude.

As Christians, we need to apply the Matthew 18 principle to our disagreements. This passage primarily deals with disagreements in the church, but it is also applicable to other areas of our lives. If you have a disagreement with someone, you are to first go and speak with them about this. You are not to talk to the teacher next door, or go to your supervisor with the issue, and especially don't discuss it in the teachers' lounge. We must confront the person privately as a first step. If that does not resolve the disagreement, then you must find someone to go with you to the person again and have them serve as a mediator in an attempt to work through the issue. In Luke 11:17, Jesus said that *"...every kingdom divided against itself is brought to desolation..."* In Genesis 11:1-9 at the Tower of Babel, God spoke about how the people could accomplish whatever they wanted because they had one speech, one language, and one goal – they were unified in how they lived and in how they acted. Unity is stressed in other passages as well. Therefore, it is important that we work diligently to resolve any conflicts or disagreements in order to maintain unity in our school.

The next quality is that we are "not self-willed." I'm sure we know many people who think the world revolves around them, and if we ask them they would tell us that is true. We are not to be self-

WANTED: Christian Educators with Character

centered and think that we are our own authority. If we were to talk about children being self-willed, we would probably say they are "spoiled." You may take that thought and apply it accordingly. I have heard teachers say "I know the administration wants us to do this, but I have a better way of doing it." Some teachers tell students that there are some school rules they will not enforce in their classroom because they don't think they are important or they don't agree with them. They are being self-willed. I have read many leadership books over the years and over and over you read statements to the effect that "to be a good leader, you must be a good follower." If you are not able to follow your administrator, why would you expect your students to follow you?

I dealt with a student one time in regard to his being tardy to school and to class. This was a consistent problem so it had come to the point of having a meeting with his parents over the issue. Unfortunately, the parent's response was a question: "Why does he have to be on time if the teacher doesn't start class on time? That's a tough question to answer because it indicates that the real problem is with the teacher, not the student. We must set the example and not be self-willed. Obviously, my next meeting was with the teacher to make sure that problem was corrected.

Another quality is to "not be contentious." A contentious person is a competitive person who always has to win or they are unhappy. When a Christian exhibits this kind of character, it disrupts the unity of the body of Christ. This, of course, can be applied to an organization as well because lack of unity disrupts the effectiveness of the organization, as we just mentioned above. We see this contentious trait in athletes. If a wide receiver doesn't get enough (in his mind) passes thrown to him in a game, he is not happy because he thinks the game is about him and not about the team. This disrupts the team. Our goal as Christian educators is to make our school successful, not to make "me" successful.

As we conclude this chapter dealing with character, may we be challenged to examine our lives carefully to determine what changes we may need to make to exhibit the character qualities that will bring glory to God. We must remember that our lives as Christians must be for God's glory, not our own.

Chapter 3

A PERSONAL SPIRITUAL PERSPECTIVE

It has often been said that you can't have a complete Christian education without having Christian educators and Christian students. I recognize that those who teach in secular schools are not able to offer a Christian education by this description, nor are all educators who teach in Christian schools, because not all students in a Christian school are Christians. However, those who teach in secular schools have opportunities to influence the thinking of their students along spiritual lines if they will take advantage of those opportunities. Those who teach in Christian schools do have the freedom to present Christ without any hindrances in every class and in every activity of the school. If the educator is not a Christian, you can definitely not provide a Christian education. If the educator is a Christian, but has unsaved students, can they offer a Christian education? I don't believe they can offer this to the unsaved students because the unsaved students are not able to understand the spiritual aspects of the education they are given because the Holy Spirit does not dwell within them. Perhaps I should clarify this by saying that a Christian teacher in a Christian school can provide a Christian education, but the unsaved student will not receive a Christian education until the Word of God that is presented convicts them and they become a Christian.

The ideal, of course, is to have a Christian educator teaching Christian students because the Holy Spirit can then intervene in the educational process. I am not necessarily advocating Covenant Christian schools (although they have their place in our society), as I believe there is benefit of accepting unsaved students into a Christian school as long as the mission of the school includes the aspect of evangelism. If you are teaching unsaved students, don't despair, but you must clearly present the Word of God so the Holy Spirit can use it in the hearts of these unsaved students to convict them of their sins so they become Christians.

We have dealt with having proper Christian character and now we will turn to dealing with a similar topic, that of having a proper spiritual perspective – "thinking" like a Christian. We will deal with a Biblical worldview in our next chapter to further elaborate on our Christian thinking. In this chapter we are going to deal with the heart aspects of Christian thinking.

Salvation

The first and most important aspect for a Christian educator is for them to be saved and to know they are saved. Unfortunately, there are many people who think they are saved because they did something at some religious service or meeting, but their life never changed. Many have learned the "lingo" of talking like a Christian but they have never made the decision to accept Christ and become a Christian.

Salvation is not complicated. God made it simple enough for everyone to understand. However, because it is so simple, many have oversimplified it to a point where it doesn't mean anything to them. Salvation takes place at a moment in time but there are some things that must take place prior to that actual moment. A person must first of all recognize they are a sinner (Romans 3:23). Unless you recognize that you are a sinner and need a Savior, you can't be saved. The next step is for you to recognize that because of your sin, you deserve to die and spend eternity in Hell (Romans 5:8). However, God loved you so much that even while you were still a sinner, He sent His Son (Jesus Christ) into this world to die in your place (Romans 5:8). God has provided the way to escape death, but you must accept it and apply it to your life in order for it to take effect. You must trust that Christ's death paid the price for your sins. If you accept this free gift of salvation, you will be saved and will not have to die, but will spend eternity in Heaven. As we speak about death, we are speaking of spiritual death, not physical death.

In Mark 10 we have the story of the rich, young ruler who came to Jesus and asked Him what he had to do to inherit eternal life. Jesus told him that he should sell all he had and give it to the poor. The man went away sorrowful because he had great possessions. The point is, not that you have to sell everything to be saved, but this man loved his money more than he loved Jesus and therefore could not be saved. Is there something in your life that is keeping you from accepting His free gift of salvation?

When we come to Jesus, nothing can be off-limits and we can't negotiate with God with pre-conditions or limitations. We must approach Him in total surrender, which is the essence of repentance. Repentance simply means "a change of mind." Some people think there are a lot of things they need to clean up in their life prior to accepting Christ, but salvation is a change of mind (heart), not a change in actions. When you change your mind about your spiritual condition (recognize that you are a sinner and realize you cannot save yourself) and accept Christ as your Savior, then you will see a change in your actions. Your actions change because of your change of mind, not the other way around.

Has your life changed after you experienced that moment of salvation? If not, you may have not come to God with a totally surrendered mind. We need to examine our hearts and determine if we are hanging on to something that is keeping us from Christ.

Before moving forward, it is important that we deal with the topic of "eternal security" or "once saved, always saved." I understand there are differences of opinion on this doctrine, but I believe it is a very important doctrine. The bottom line is that we cannot do anything to lose our salvation once we are saved (John 10:28-29). Yes, we will sin, because we are born with a sin nature, and when we receive our new spiritual nature, the old sinful nature does not leave us; it still influences us. However, if we are truly saved, we will not have peace if we continue in sin.

Your Calling to Ministry

As a Christian educator, are you doing what God has called you to do? There are many reasons for Christians to teach. Some get a job in a Christian school so their children will receive a "tuition-free" Christian education. Others teach because someone once told them that they would be a good teacher. There are many other reasons, but the most important reason that we should teach is that God has called us to teach and to minister to the students (and their parents) He will put in our classes.

I supervised a teacher one time who survived her first year of teaching (barely) and really struggled in the first quarter of the second year. When a meeting was held to discuss her issues, I asked the question – "Do you enjoy teaching?" Her response very quickly indicated the problem when she said "I really love the children." Even though she had spent four years in college studying to be a teacher, she did not have a calling to be a teacher – she did it because she loved children. That's not a good enough reason, especially when the children don't behave as we want them to. Please don't misunderstand, I believe that teachers should love children, but there is so much more than just loving children in the calling to be a teacher.

For those who have been teaching for any length of time, we recognize that we are going to have days when we are ready to quit teaching, but because it is a calling, we rely on God to get us through that situation. If we were not called, it would be much easier to quit in the middle of a problem. When God calls us to minister to others, in whatever capacity, He will give us the grace and strength needed to fulfill that calling as long as we rely on Him.

If you teach in a Christian school, the importance of a calling is even more important because of the ministry aspect of the school. Many Christian schools are focused on an evangelistic aspect of sharing the gospel with their students and parents. A part of the school's mission is to win the students to Christ and to disciple them to become followers of Christ. There are other Christian schools that are called "covenant" schools that only accept students who are a part of a Christian family, with at least one parent/guardian who is a Christian and who regularly attends church. Therefore, their focus is more on the discipleship aspect than the evangelistic aspect. However, discipleship is definitely something a Christian should feel called to do, in addition to their teaching.

If you teach in a secular school as a Christian, I believe that is still a calling and it is a ministry. You have the opportunity to influence many children or young people with your testimony and your character. In today's society, people want you to think that you can't mention God or anything to do with God at any time in a secular school. That is not true and there are books written on this topic as well as organizations whose chief goal is to help Christian educators in public schools to know how to share their faith. I trust you will search these out to enable you to be effective in this area of your calling. May I refer you to two resources that I believe will be informative and helpful:

1) Van Brummelen, H. (2009). *Walking with God in the Classroom.* Colorado Springs, CO: Purposeful Designs. ISBN: 978-1-58331-098-4

2) Gateway to Better Education (www.gtbe.org)

Daily Living and Growing

When you think about living a Christian life, what thoughts come to your mind? For some, you immediately think about the rules you have to obey in order to appear spiritual – rules about dress, rules about what activities you can participate in, and the list goes on and on. For others, there are certain rituals you must keep – reading your Bible, praying, going to church, and others. If we don't keep these rules or follow these rituals, we feel a sense of guilt because we know we can do better. We assume that God is not happy with us because we're not doing our best to live as a Christian should (or at least how we have been taught a Christian should live). Is that really what the Christian life is all about?

In Matthew 22:34-40, the Pharisees asked Jesus what the greatest commandment was. His response was that if you love God and you love others, you have satisfied the commandments and the rest of the Christian life falls naturally into place. The question then is how can we learn to love God? We understand that love grows as a response to the loveliness of the object of our love. This is why the Holy Spirit works in our hearts to show us the loveliness of God through His Word which builds our desire for God. 1 John 4:19 tells us that we love Him because He first loved us. We know it is much easier to love someone if they already love us.

John 15:9 says, *"As the Father loved Me, I also have loved you; abide in My love."* Have you considered what it means to "abide?" The basic meaning of "abide" is "to make your home in." Think about it, we are to make our home in God's love! If we do this, we will produce spiritual fruit of which our daily Christian living is a part. We know that we are supposed to produce spiritual fruit in our Christian lives since we have the Holy Spirit living in us. Galatians 5 tells us that the fruit of the Spirit is spiritual fruit, and it starts with love. How do we go about producing that spiritual fruit? What does spiritual fruit look like?

I believe that J.D. Greer (2011) helps us understand this by making an interesting comparison between physical fruit and spiritual fruit. He says,

> Spiritual 'fruit,' you see, is produced in the same way physical 'fruit' is. When a man and woman conceive physical 'fruit' (i.e., a child), they are usually not thinking about the mechanics of making that child. Rather, they get caught up in the moment of loving intimacy with one another, and the fruit of that loving intimacy is a child. In the same way, spiritual fruit isn't made by focusing on the commands of spiritual growth....So if you want to see spiritual fruit in your life, don't focus primarily on the fruits. Focus on Jesus' acceptance of you, given to you as a gift (p. 13).

Our focus then, is to be on Christ, not on keeping rules or rituals. We are not commanded to bear fruit, however, we are commanded to abide in Christ. The unique result of abiding in Christ is that we will produce spiritual fruit. If we are in "love" with Christ, we won't have to worry about whether or not we read our Bible today because when we are in love, we want to spend time with that person. The way we spend time with Christ is to read His Word and talk to Him in prayer. That should be a liberating thought for many of us who have been trying to obey the rules and follow the rituals without thinking about our abiding in Christ.

So, we know what to do – love the Lord with all our heart, soul, and mind and to love our neighbor as ourselves. However, where do we get the power to do this? We find that the Holy Spirit gives us that power as we read God's Word and as we grow in our desire to love God. If you have been trying to be obedient to what you know God wants you to do without the love, you are probably frustrated and wondering if it's worth the effort. However, when you change that focus to loving God, the same obedience becomes a delight.

The sin of Adam and Eve was a form of idolatry because they put their desire for the tree ahead of their desire for God. When we sin, we find the same thing in our lives – we sin because we desire something more than we desire God. Trying to change our behavior (i.e., I'll read my Bible 30 minutes a day now instead of the 10 minutes I've been spending) is not successful because we haven't addressed the root problem of our idolatry of not loving God. We also find that trying to change our behavior doesn't work because then our focus is on our performance, not on loving God. We try to do more to make ourselves more acceptable to God. Don't ever forget Ephesians 2:8-9: *"For by grace you have been saved through faith, and that not of yourselves; it is the gift of God, not of works, lest anyone should boast."* This passage very clearly states that we are saved by grace and not by works. It is our love for Christ, not what we do and how we behave. I knew a man once that realized that while he was on his way to church he actually went 5 mph over the speed limit (This is not confession time for all of us!). He felt guilty and felt he needed to do something about this, so on the way home he went 5 mph under the speed limit. We may laugh at this, but how many times have we done a similar thing trying to correct our sins? We try to balance the scale with good and bad, hoping we can please God that way. Another question that arises when we try to gain acceptance from God by changing our behavior is: When have we done enough? How many times a week do we have to go to church? How many minutes do I have to spend reading the Bible? How much money do I have to give to the church, and to missions, and to the poor, etc. etc. etc. My advice is: Learn to love God, obedience will come. It's not about what you do, it's about you loving God.

I recently re-read the book *The Pursuit of Holiness* by Jerry Bridges (1996) and was reminded of a number of things associated with this principle of our daily living and growing. If you had to describe how a person can become holy, what would you say? Do we have to do something? Or does it relate to our discussion above in regard to developing our love and passion for God which then leads to holiness. You may even be wondering if a person can become holy in our society today.

I grew up on a farm and came to realize at an early age that a farmer can only do so much in an effort to produce crops. Our major crop was corn. To produce a good crop of corn, you have to prepare the field by plowing and discing to break up the hard soil. Then you can plant, but then you have to cultivate and fertilize. However, you never know until harvest time if you will harvest or not. A farmer can't make it rain and he can't stop it from raining too much. I have seen corn crops ruined by a late summer hail storm and that means there will be no harvest that year because the stalks are stripped. The farmer is in partnership with God and he will reap the harvest if he does his part and God does His part. God is in charge of the rain and the sunshine and the farmer has to depend on God after he has done his part of preparing the soil and planting. Bridges (1996) says, "Farming is a joint venture between God and the farmer. The *farmer cannot do* what God must do, and *God will not do* what the farmer should do" (p. 9).

How does this relate to holiness? To develop holiness, we have a responsibility to do what we need to do and God will do the rest. However, He will not do in us what we are supposed to do. Too many times we say and we act like it's totally up to God and I'm just going to sit and wait for Him to work. That's not God's plan. I realize that this may seem like a contradiction to what I've said above in regard to our relationship with God is not based on what we do. However, I also said that we must develop our relationship with God. With the human relationships you have, you realize that they don't begin, nor do they grow, if we don't work on building them. We are talking in this section about building our relationship, not about our salvation or gaining favor with God.

Much of what we talked about above relates to this concept, but I'd like to sharpen the focus in this section. If we are going to talk about being holy, we need to clarify the definition so we know to what we are referring. Holiness is defined as "to be morally blameless." We are instructed in 1 Peter 1:15-16, *"But just as He who called you is holy, so be holy in all you do; for it is written: 'Be holy, because I am holy.'"* WOW! That means that we are commanded to be holy! It doesn't take too long for most of us (I will include myself in this category) to realize that we fall extremely short of that so we wonder if it's even worth the effort.

One of our problems is that our attitude toward sin is more self-centered than God-centered. We think that when we stop committing a sin, we have done a great thing because we got victory over it. However, that means it was us who did it and not God. Our attitude should be, as stated in the Beattitudes (Matthew 5:4), that we should grieve (mourn) over our sin because it is what sent Christ to the cross. God wants us to be obedient because obedience is directed toward Him, not us. We also don't take some sin seriously. We have classified sins into the ones that are not so bad, others that are bad, and others that are really bad. However, God doesn't classify sin and if we desire to be holy, we must follow His classification system – all sin is equally bad. We know, although we won't always admit it, that when we compromise with the "little" sins, it usually leads to compromise on "bigger" sins. We must be willing to call sin "sin" regardless of how we categorize it.

I believe many Christians have changed the standard of holiness for themselves and define it in a way that they can adjust their standard based on the society around them. They see society change and they change with it instead of remaining steadfast to the standard God has established for us. We have been taught that holiness is one of God's attributes and we know that God doesn't change, which means holiness doesn't change either. Many times we give in to pressures around us and even though we know what the right thing to do is, we don't do it because of the circumstances in which we find ourselves. Obviously, God doesn't have this problem because He is omniscient and never has any questions about what is right or wrong.

We know God is holy and, therefore, He hates sin (Proverbs 6:16-19). Do we realize then, that every time we sin, we are doing something God hates? We are sometimes so used to our sins that we don't even think about them being wrong. However, the next time you are tempted to do something wrong, think about the fact that God hates what you are about to do. Will that change your decision to do it? We rationalize in our minds that we will only do it one time and surely there won't be great consequences if we do it just one time. However, think about Moses. Because he was disobedient one time by striking the rock instead of speaking to it to get water (Numbers 20:7-12), he was not allowed to enter the Promised Land. We know that was not his only sin, but think about how faithful he was for all of those years, and yet because of one act of disobedience, he suffered the consequences. Why do we think we can get away with disobedience and not have to suffer any consequences?

We know that we cannot be holy by our own merits because Isaiah 64:6 tells us that all our righteousness is as filthy rags. When we consider Romans 3:10-18 and the indictment Paul writes for all mankind, we wonder how in the world we can be holy or even think about being holy. The solution, of course, is our life in Christ. When we accepted Christ as our personal Savior, we were given Christ's righteousness. Bridges (1996) says, "...we are through Christ *made* holy in our standing before God, and *called* to be holy in our daily lives" (p. 33). In Ephesians 1:4, Paul tells us that God chose us so we would be holy and blameless before Him. Paul also states that *"I have been crucified with Christ; it is no longer I who lives, but Christ lives in me; and the life which I now live in the flesh I live by faith in the Son of God, who loved me and gave Himself for me"* (Galatians 2:20).

I would encourage you to read Psalm 15. David begins the Psalm with a question regarding who is able to dwell in God's tabernacle and dwell with Him. In the following verses he answers this question by telling us the character of such a person. A basic summary of these verses tells us that such a person must live a holy life.

"God does not require a perfect, sinless life to have fellowship with Him, but He does require that we be serious about holiness, that we grieve over sin in our lives instead of justifying it, and that we earnestly pursue holiness as a way of life" (Bridges, 1996, p. 36).

I would be remiss if I close this section without again expressing the purpose of our holiness in relation to being a Christian educator. As a Christian educator, we are to be examples of Christ to our students and their families. If we don't display holiness to them, are we really being effective as a Christian? How are they going to see the holiness of God if we are not holy? Can we fulfill our calling if we do not love God as we should and therefore do not live holy lives?

Chapter 4

A BIBLICAL WORLDVIEW

[Much of the material in this section has been gleaned from Colson & Pearcey, 1996; Pearcey, 2005; and Johnson, 2002 from a recent study I did on Biblical worldview.]

We have looked at the importance of having a proper heart in regard to being an effective "Christian" educator. However, having the right heart is not the only pre-requisite. In this chapter we will examine the importance of having a proper Biblical worldview.

Everyone has a worldview and our worldview is shaped by our parents, our education, our experiences, our exposure to events around us, our culture, and many other factors. Unfortunately, much of the world around us is anti-Biblical and this tends to taint our worldview as Christians. Christians must be diligent to develop a Biblical worldview so they are able to live and teach from this perspective.

A number of years ago, the Barna Research Group conducted a survey to find out how many people had a Biblical worldview. They replicated the study a couple of years later to validate their findings. Their conclusion was that "a large share of the nation's moral and spiritual challenges is directly attributable to the absence of a Biblical worldview among Americans" (Barna, 2003, p.1). They found that only 4% of adults have a Biblical worldview and only 9% of born again Christians have such a perspective.

> For the purposes of the research, a biblical worldview was defined as believing that absolute moral truths exist; that such truth is defined by the Bible; and having a firm belief in six specific religious views. Those views were that Jesus Christ lived a sinless life; God is the all-powerful and all-knowing Creator of the universe and He still rules it today; salvation is a gift from God and cannot be earned; Satan is real; a Christian has a responsibility to share their faith in Christ with other people; and the Bible is accurate in all of its teachings (Barna, 2003, p.2).

Christian educators in Christian schools have the opportunity to teach Biblical information since daily Bible classes are usually required, Chapels are usually held weekly for the students, and the Bible is integrated into all subject matter to give a Biblical perspective. However, do we teach the students how this information fits into their daily lives? Perhaps we should also ask, do we, as educators, know how to fit this information into our daily lives? Many of our students come from secular homes or nominally Christian homes and they are drastically impacted by all of the media exposure, especially the social media. How do they apply what we teach them in their daily lives? Do most of them just have a "Christian" corner in their lives that doesn't intersect the other areas of their lives? Do we even know how to teach them in a way that will help them apply the Bible to their lives?

A major concern in this, of course, is whether their teachers (that's us!) are showing them, by example, how it all fits together. If the Christian educator does not have a Biblical worldview, or does not live according to a Biblical worldview, or does not teach from a Biblical worldview perspective, there is no way the students will develop such a worldview and live accordingly. If their parents have a Biblical worldview and live according to that worldview, the student has a much better chance of developing their own Biblical worldview. Gaebelein (1968) states that the problem with providing a God-centered education in our schools falls primarily on the educators. (This is not as true with secular school educators because the philosophy of the administration in a secular school typically is not conducive to this type of teaching. However, Christian educators in secular schools should still have a Biblical worldview.) Gaebelein (1968) says,

> "The fact is inescapable; the world view of the educator, in so far as he is effective, gradually conditions the world view of the pupil...every educator expresses the convictions he lives by, whether they be spiritually positive or negative" (p. 37).

The culture in which we live is morally indifferent, or perhaps we could even say it is anti-moral. The culture mocks most of the values that Christians consider important and the culture ignores morality, for the most part. However, they seem to hold those who differ from their opinions to a higher standard. I am sure there are times when you have just wanted to escape from this culture and find a deserted island on which to live (at least for a few hours). However, as Christians, we have a responsibility to redeem our culture, not turn our backs on it, and definitely not to agree with it.

It's interesting that individual autonomy, the right to do what one chooses, has not produced the freedom everyone thought it would. Instead, we have found that it produces chaos and a loss of civility. Our society is now searching for something that will help us make sense of our lives, since our living with choice without morality has caused such chaos. As Christians, we have the answer to this search and we need to share it with others in a way that is relevant to their everyday lives. That answer is a Biblical worldview. Too many times we think that a Biblical worldview is only what we believe on our "Christian side" of life and we don't apply it to our entire life. We must understand that our beliefs are to govern everything we do in every area of our life.

Colson & Pearcey (1999) discuss the major conflicts in our culture today and I will summarize their discussion regarding Christianity vs. Naturalism because I believe it gives us a clearer picture of our need of developing a Biblical worldview. They say, "Theism is the belief that there is a transcendent God who created the universe; naturalism is the belief that natural causes alone are sufficient to explain everything that exists" (p. 20). Notice how the differences between the two begin with the concept of creation.

If nature is all there is, there is no source for moral truth which means everyone gets to decide what is moral or not moral based on their preferences. (Does this sound like your community?) This leads to what we call moral relativism, which is rampant in today's society. Moral relativism leads to postmodernism or multiculturalism because if there is no source for truth or morality, we have to find our basis for living in other things, which typically means we resort to identifying ourselves based on our race, gender, ethnic group, or lifestyle. However, as Christians, we believe in absolute truth and morality as defined in the Scriptures. Therefore, by our nature as Christians, since we have these absolutes, we end up judging the morality of these culture groups based on absolute truth. This is not appreciated by these cultural groups, nor by society in general, because they say it makes us intolerant toward their viewpoints.

Naturalists tend to take a pragmatic view of life which says "whatever works best is right." Again, this comes from their belief that there are no moral absolutes. Christians, on the other hand, judge actions based on objective truths found in the Bible, not by what works, or what seems to be right. It's no surprise that naturalists believe that the human nature is essentially good, which leads to utopianism. As Christian educators, we have a hard time accepting the thought that the human nature is essentially good, because we know the students that come into our classrooms on a daily basis and they are not essentially good! If you ask any parent, they will tell you that one thing they didn't have to teach their child was how to do wrong. As Christians, we believe that sin is real and we believe that it affects human nature. We observe this on a daily basis in our schools and in our communities. How can anyone believe that our human nature is essentially good when we have so much crime in our communities and so many problems in our schools. As Christians, we must realize that our human nature can only be controlled by the truths and the principles which are established in the Scriptures as we are empowered by the Holy Spirit.

As we continue to consider the conflict between Christians and naturalists, we come to the point that naturalists only see life as it exists in this world and they believe that when they die, it's over. However, as Christians, we realize that life has an eternal perspective and how we live now does have eternal significance because we will one day be judged based on our choices in this life.

How has naturalism affected your school? If you are in a secular school, you have been told that you can't talk about God, you can't celebrate the "Christian" holidays, you can't pray at public events, and the list goes on with all of the restrictions. The reason for this is, the naturalists don't want any of the Christian moral standards affecting their individual practices. However, in a Christian school, we have freedom to discuss right and wrong from a Biblical perspective. However, have you seen your Christian school avoid some practices today that used to be a part of the school because they don't want to offend some of their parents, or they don't enforce certain standards that they use to enforce because too many parents have complained? I'm not saying that we should never change our practices because I think you have to continually evaluate what you are doing, how you are doing it, and why you are doing it. However, I am saying that you should never change your practices if those practices are based on the truth and morality of God's Word. An example of this would be the changing of standards in so many Christian colleges. The standard in most Christian colleges was total abstinence from alcohol. Over the last ten years, many Christian colleges have changed that standard and now allow their faculty and students to drink alcohol.

I have seen Christian schools take a stand on some issues where others would not take such a stand. They took this stand in spite of the complaints from some of the parents, in spite of disagreement among faculty as to what should be done, and in spite of the consequences which had to be administered. A couple of these areas would deal with the issues of drugs and alcohol. Also, in today's society there are issues of what students are sharing via social media, such as sexting. I believe that when we stand for what is right and for the truth, God will bless our school. If we don't take a Biblical stand and if we compromise our Biblical position, I don't believe God will bless us. That should cause us to be cautious in regard to changing our practices. We must keep them aligned with Biblical principles.

I am writing this chapter on the weekend of July 4th and we have been reminded once again of what our founding fathers said and did as they established our nation and our governmental system. However, people today are denying that our nation was founded on Judeo-Christian truths and principles. One commentator said that, as a nation, we have deviated from our principles because we aren't teaching our students the true history of our country anymore. What will it take? If you teach in the social studies area of your school, do you clearly communicate the basics of the founding of our country? Do you emphasize the importance our founding fathers placed on their reliance upon God as they made their decisions? We need to take our country back to our original values (notice that I did not say practices, I said values), and one way of doing this is to teach history from a Biblical worldview perspective, regardless of the opinions of others (naturalists).

The term "naturalist" may not be familiar to you, but you may have heard the word "postmodernism" which is a synonym. "Postmodernism rejects any notion of a universal, overarching truth and reduces all ideas to social constructions shaped by class, gender, and ethnicity" (Colson & Pearcey, 1999, p. 23). They are resistant to any or all truth, not just Biblical truth. This movement began with the existentialists who claim that life is meaningless and you establish meaning in your own life by your own choices. In postmodernism, all viewpoints, all lifestyles, all beliefs, and all behaviors are regarded as equally valid. However, do they really believe that? We are finding that they do believe that, as long as you agree with them, but if you disagree, you will not be accepted as having a valid belief. How can we be wrong if all viewpoints are equally valid and there are no absolutes? We are finding colleges that will not allow anyone to speak that may have a different opinion than the "so-called public opinion." In doing this, they are denying their own belief that everyone gets to choose what is right for them. Choice seems to be a great thing when it applies to me, but not when it applies to you – unless you agree with me.

I know as we consider these thoughts and as we watch our society decline into a culture of seemingly not believing anything, it can be easy to get discouraged and wonder if it isn't just easier to give in and join them instead of standing firm on the truth and the principles of Scripture. However, don't ever forget – the Truth will ultimately prevail and the Truth will set you free!

I have laid out these thoughts above for several reasons, but most of all to convince us (or at least remind us) that it is essential for us to develop our own Biblical worldview that is established from the truths from God's Word and then to defend that worldview. As we develop our Biblical worldview, we cannot be concerned about being politically correct; we must be concerned about being Biblically correct. It is important to have some understanding of the opposing worldviews, and why people believe them, which helps us better able to combat them. Coaches of athletic teams spend considerable time studying the opposing teams to determine what their tendencies are, and what their strengths and weaknesses are. This enables the coach to put a game plan together for his team based on the knowledge he has about his own team to expose the weaknesses of the other team when they get into a game.

From that perspective, do you know enough about what you believe (the strengths of your own team) to even put a game plan together? Have you even thought about the opposing worldviews in order to determine how you are going to stand against them? I would say that we have all probably faced this opposition in some form – how have we handled it? If our students from Christian schools go to a secular college, are they prepared by knowing what they believe (the truth), why they believe it, and how they can defend it? Are they prepared to raise questions when topics come up in class that contradict what they believe? Are we prepared to answer questions that are raised to us from others in our society? Peter tells us *"...always be ready to give a defense to everyone who asks you a reason for the hope that is in you..."* (1 Peter 3:15). Do you know what you believe well enough to defend it to those who question it?

I know some will ask about the difference between a Christian worldview and a Biblical worldview. Is there a difference? My response would be that there should be no difference, but it depends on your definition of a Christian. If your definition of a Christian includes the concept that a Christian believes and lives by the truths and principles of the Word of God, I would say the two concepts are the same. However, we know that many people today call themselves Christians, but they don't believe parts of the Bible and they don't believe they have to live a certain way because they say the Bible is old-fashioned. I would say their "Christian" worldview is not a "Biblical worldview." I prefer the term "Biblical" because if you are holding to the truths of God's Word, you are solidly grounded.

Every worldview basically looks at three questions, and how a person answers these questions determines the worldview they develop. The three questions are:

1. Creation: Where did we come from and who are we?

2. Fall: What has gone wrong with the world?

3. Redemption: What can we do to fix it?

These questions sound so simple, so why does a Biblical worldview seem so complicated? It seems complicated because we have basically separated our lives into two domains – the spiritual and the secular – and we typically don't mix the two. However, our life is one life and we can't be dividing it between the spiritual and the secular. We have to stand for the same truths and morality on Monday when we go to school or work as we did on Sunday when we went to church. We must understand that the Bible clearly answers these questions and we need to know these Biblical answers which will result in a Biblical worldview.

Creation:

Genesis 1 states that God created the heavens and the earth and we have been taught that God spoke everything into existence out of nothing (ex nihilo). John tells us in John 1 that Christ made the world and nothing was made that He did not make. Therefore, consider this thought: Everything that exists came into being at His command and is therefore subject to Him, and finds its purpose and meaning in Him. Paul further develops this thought in Colossians 1:16-18 where he speaks of the preeminence of Christ and says that *"all things were created through Him and for Him."*

We have heard the statement that "all truth is God's truth." Pilate even asks the question, *"What is truth?"* (John 18:38) when he was interrogating Jesus prior to the crucifixion. What is interesting to note is that Jesus had already described truth in John 14:6 when He said, *"I am the way, the truth, and the life."* If Jesus is the truth and He created everything, then everything is subject to Him and we should recognize that every aspect of our lives must fall under His control, not just the spiritual side of our lives. We must see the Bible (the Truth) as the root of everything we do.

Our society thinks there are no consequences for what they do because they see themselves as gods and capable of deciding what is right and wrong for themselves. However, we know that if you try to ignore any of the physical laws, for example, the law of gravity, that doesn't change the fact that gravity will still control you. You cannot ignore it. Every action against a physical law results in a predictable reaction because physical laws don't change. Similarly, certain moral behaviors produce predictable consequences, even if we think we are above these and don't have to live by them. You cannot transgress the moral law without consequences.

Consider the life of David. We know that he chose to commit adultery with Bathsheba and when she became pregnant he went to great lengths to have her husband killed so he could take her as his wife. After about a year, when confronted by Nathan the prophet, David repented of his sin and asked for forgiveness (2 Samuel 12). You can read his prayer of confession in Psalm 51 to get a sense of his remorse. However, David suffered the consequences of this immoral decision for the rest of his life. God told him that the sword would never depart from his house. The child that he fathered with Bathsheba died, his children became immoral and fought with one another to the point of murder. You cannot transgress the moral law without consequences. In dealing with discipline over the years, I've had many students who would admit when they were wrong and ask for forgiveness and expect that to free them from any consequences. They were of the opinion that if they were forgiven, everything was okay. We must understand that we are thankful for forgiveness, but we must still pay the consequences. Some teachers will use the expression, "It's easier to ask for forgiveness than permission." However, there are still consequences for acting without permission.

If our desire is to live well-balanced lives, we must know the laws by which God structured creation. The understanding of these laws is what the Bible calls wisdom. "A wise person is one who knows the boundaries and limits, the laws and rhythms and seasons of the created order, both in the physical and the social world" (Colson & Pearcey, 1999, p. 16).

I trust that this discussion helps you consider your position in regard to the first question of establishing your worldview in regard to creation. Our next question deals with the fall – what has gone wrong with the world?

Fall:

When Christians consider the fall, our minds typically go back to the Garden of Eden where Adam and Eve committed the first sin. However, many Christians and seculars alike question this entire scenario. Why would a wise and good God create a perfect world and allow evil to exist? In the account of creation in Genesis 1 we read that each day when God made something it is recorded that "*... God saw that it was good...*" (Genesis 1:3, 9, 12, 18, 21, 25). Genesis concludes the account of creation with the statement "*Then God saw everything that He had made, and indeed it was very good*" (Genesis 1:31). So, if all of creation was "very good," why would God allow evil to come into the world? The Bible clearly teaches us that God created the universe and then created man in His image and created man to be holy and to commune with God without any interference. However, God didn't want to "require" man to worship Him (like a robot would). He wanted man to have the option of "choosing" to worship Him.

When God created Adam and Eve, He gave them only one moral restriction which was they were not to eat of the tree of knowledge of good and evil. Use your imagination to picture the conditions under which Adam and Eve lived in the Garden. They had been placed in charge of caring for the Garden. We know that Adam named all of the animals. They spent time each evening walking with God in the Garden. They had work to do but there was no sweat because of their work! They cared for the Garden but there were no weeds to pull and the flowers were always in bloom. What an environment!

They were able to live in these "utopian" conditions and to live their lives as they chose, with only one restriction. Adam and Eve chose to sin and break that one restriction so consequences had to follow. They chose to disobey God. We need to understand that obedience is not just an external act; it is an internal response to God. God did not give them this restriction as a "rule" but His desire was to build a relationship. He wants us to love Him with our entire being because we choose to do so. Scripture teaches us that God established a "valid standard of right and wrong. Our choice has no effect at all on this standard; our choice simply determines whether we accept it, or reject it, and suffer the consequences" (Colson & Pearcey, 1999, p. 194).

We discussed above the fact that God is good and that creation was good. If that is true, from where did evil come? We know that Eve was tempted by a very powerful spiritual being (Satan) who questioned God's authority. Remember why Satan was cast out of Heaven? He wanted to be like God (Isaiah 14:14). This is the same tactic he used with Eve. He first asked "Did God really say" you couldn't eat of any tree in the Garden? In Eve's response, she added a few words to what God had instructed them as she said that they could eat of any tree except the tree that was in the middle of the Garden, and they couldn't even touch it, or they would die. God had not told them they could not touch it, only that they could not eat of it. Adding things to God's Word is a first step in a decline in our spiritual life. Satan was then ready and he confronted her truth, that they could not eat of it, with a lie – *"You will not surely die"* (Genesis 3:4). He goes further and says that not only will they not die, but they will become like God.

The sin of Adam and Eve was not the eating of the fruit – it was a desire to have godlike power. They wanted something that was not theirs to have. They wanted to be their own god. Does that sound familiar? Isn't that what we discussed above with the philosophy of the world today where everyone gets to choose what is right and wrong for themselves, which makes them their own god. Because of Adam and Eve's sin, everyone from that point forward has been born with a sin nature which gives us a natural tendency to do wrong things. As I mentioned earlier, there are some who try to convince us that man is inherently good and will do good if left to himself. However, we know from Scripture that is not true.

Many people have a hard time accepting the thought of everyone being born with a sin nature, not because they don't understand it, but because they don't want to accept it. It doesn't fit with their thinking that man is inherently good. If man evolved through nature, as they believe, they have no moral guilt, but if they are born with a sin nature they do have that moral guilt.

We have been warned of this same thing happening today that happened to Adam and Eve with Satan's deceit. Peter says, *"Be sober, be vigilant; because your adversary the devil walks about like a roaring lion, seeking whom he may devour"* (1 Peter 5:8). Jesus tells us that we must be careful because Satan's mode of operation is deceit (John 8:44 *"He is a liar and the father of lies"*). We must be careful that we don't get drawn in by Satan as he tries to entice us to do evil.

Too many times we think that sin is just breaking the rules. However, it is much more than that. We must understand that sin disrupts our fellowship with God. Remember one of the first things Adam and Eve did after they had sinned? They tried to hide from God because of their guilt. Sin also alienates us from each other – remember that they covered themselves so they wouldn't be seen naked. When God confronted Adam and Eve with what they had done, Adam immediately blamed Eve (and God indirectly) and Eve blamed the serpent. We see this over and over in our society as no one wants to take responsibility for their own sin – they try to find someone they can blame for it. A third result of sin is that it affected all of nature. Adam and Eve were given control over all of creation and because of their rebellion, disorder occurred in all of creation. The earth was now going to produce thorns and thistles (as a farmer, I hated thistles!). Childbearing would result in pain and work would now be drudgery.

The culmination of this was that when man dies he would return to dust. Death would become part of the human experience.

The fall impacted every aspect of the nature of man and that's why our nature is referred to as being totally depraved. Total depravity "means that every part of our being – intellect, will, emotions, and body – shows the effects of sin. No part remains untouched by the Fall" (Colson & Pearcey, 1996, p. 198).

Redemption:

We have seen that God's creation was very good when He created it. However, we have also seen that the Fall changed everything; and we now live in a sinful world with a sinful nature. Redemption is the restoration and fulfillment of God's original purposes. Redemption is the only way the problem can be fixed and this is our focus in this section.

Let's consider for a moment where the world looks for redemption because it is definitely not the same place Christians look. Much of the world looks to science for redemption because of the logical explanation (evolution) they think it gives to the origin of the universe, but they forget that their logic is flawed because they cannot reproduce what they believe. The scientific method clearly states that you begin with a hypothesis and then you test that hypothesis by doing further testing to develop your theory. As you consider either creation or evolution, neither can be tested, because they cannot be repeated. Even if you accept the "Big Bang Theory" of the origin of the universe instead of creation, it cannot be repeated. Some look to power, money, and sex as an answer to their problems. However, if they achieve these, they soon realize there is still no satisfaction because there is always a desire for more of whatever they have. Others look to various religions, most of which are associated with the Eastern religions, but they don't find a peace there either.

WANTED: Christian Educators with Character

The only real answers to the basic questions of life are found in Christianity and the redemption found in Jesus Christ. If you want a true diagnosis of the human dilemma, you must go to the Scriptures. Scripture tells us that we have all sinned and fall short of the glory of God (Romans 3:23). We fall short because of the Fall and we are alienated from God. Regardless of what attracts us to Christianity, we must all come to a realization that we are guilty before God. We must admit that we are sinners because of the fall.

We also know that the only answer to the problem of sin is found in the Bible. Since it is human beings who sin, only a human can pay the penalty for our sin. From the other perspective, our sin offends a holy God who is infinite; and therefore, the penalty is infinite and can only be paid by God. God, in His love for us, sent His only Son, Jesus Christ, to be born as a human, to live a sinless life on earth, so He could die on the cross and pay this price. God's solution is remarkable because the substitutionary atonement permits God to be both "just and the one who justifies" (Romans 3:26).

It is also important that God's offer of salvation is based on historical fact, not on some thought that someone had. Christ's death can be pinpointed to a specific time and place. His resurrection can also be proven by historical fact. It was recognized by the soldiers who were guarding the tomb; it was proved by the fact that Christ appeared to over 500 eyewitnesses following His resurrection; it was proved by the fact of the changed lives of His disciples who refused to renounce Christ even though it meant persecution and even death. Christ's resurrection is a proven fact, and therefore, we can be assured of the fact of the availability of redemption through Christ.

If you have been a Christian for any length of time, you know the term redemption refers to our salvation. To redeem means "to buy back" which gives us the idea of someone being kidnaped and then the paying a ransom to buy them back and restoring them to their original position. God created us, but Satan kidnaped us with the fall, and then God bought us back by having Christ pay the ransom price for us. What an amazing thought when we stop and consider that. Unfortunately, many only think about this concept during the Easter season when we remember the crucifixion and resurrection of Christ.

It is important for a Christian educator to have a Biblical worldview. We must base our view of everything we teach and everything we live on the Scriptures and interpret it correctly. I challenge each of us to put our personal Biblical worldview in writing in our own words so it will stick with us and we will have that solid foundation on which to live and to teach.

Chapter 5

A LIFE OF INTEGRITY

I realize that I have already discussed the character that a Christian educator should have. However, I feel that I need to address integrity as a separate issue because of its importance in our lives as we strive to be the educator God wants us to be.

I read a story a number of years ago about a young architect who had just graduated from college and was hired by a large firm. For his first job he was assigned to design and build a house on a lot the company had purchased. He set about the task and designed the house and received the approval of the company to proceed with the construction. As he worked with the contractor, the contractor started suggesting cost saving ideas in the building that would not be noticeable to anyone, but would be flaws in the structure. The young architect resisted at first, but then realized that he could make some extra money by making these structural changes as he worked with the contractor. When the house was completely built, the owner of the architectural firm came by to inspect the house. It passed inspection and the young architect was praised for the good job he did. At that point, the owner gave the young architect the keys to the house and told him that this was his gift for doing such a good job. Don't you think the young architect now wished he hadn't made those shortcuts in the construction? He now owned the house that he didn't build to meet the specifications.

What a great lesson for us to learn from this story in regard to so many decisions we make that seemingly won't affect anyone, but later we realize they do hurt other people and sometimes ourselves. From time to time we are all faced with decisions similar to this. Sometimes we resist for a period of time but we wear down and think that everyone else is doing it, so why shouldn't I get away with it also. As Christian educators, we are to be an example to our students, as well as to their parents, and our colleagues. If we start cutting corners, what kind of an example are we? I have observed students in physical education classes be instructed to run around the gym or around a field and not to cut corners. If the teacher looks the other way, a number of students will cut the corners. Is that the type of student you want to have to depend on? Where have you cut corners in your life or in your teaching ministry? It's important to live a life of integrity so people can trust us in all aspects of our lives.

I had the opportunity several years ago to have one of my former students become my pastor and my boss. In our first meeting after he became my pastor, I told him that I hoped that I had done a good job of teaching him so he would be the right kind of a boss. Think about it – one of the students in your class may one day be your boss. Are you training them properly so they have integrity and will be a good leader?

The word "integrity" is found in Scripture between 20 and 30 times, depending on which translation you use. The words that are used in some translations to replace integrity are "upright," "blameless," and "without reproach."

According to the International Standard Bible Encyclopedia (1979), the basic meaning of "integrity" in the OT is "soundness of character and adherence to moral principle," i.e., uprightness and honesty...A common expression is "to walk in integrity," indicating an habitual manner of life. In Proverbs, integrity is seen as an essential characteristic of the upright life: Yahweh [God] will protect those who walk in it (2:7); their security is assured (2:21; 10:9; 20:7; 28:18); it is a trustworthy guide for living (11:3), and it is better than wealth (19:1; 28:6).

I think the comment about "walking in integrity," having the idea of "a habitual manner of life" is a great thought. Integrity becomes a habit in our lives as we walk in integrity. If you had a number of your friends and family members interviewed for the purpose of their answering the main question of "Does [your name] live a life of integrity?" what would their responses be?

Stephen Covey (1989) challenged his readers to do an exercise to help them develop character in their lives. He asked each one to pretend they went to a funeral and when they arrived, they found out it was their own funeral. The pastor spoke for a while and then asked several people to come forward and share their thoughts about you. This is a rather scary thought, but the exercise was to write out what you would like for each of them to say about you, not what you thought they would say. If you know what you want them to say about you, the challenge is to begin living that way now so they can say it when the time comes.

I referred to Psalm 15 earlier, but I want to look at this passage more closely. The question is asked, "Lord, who may abide in Your tabernacle? Who may dwell in Your holy hill?" When you think about the tabernacle from an Old Testament perspective, this is where God dwelt. In the tabernacle was a special piece of furniture called the Ark of the Covenant and that was God's dwelling place. After the construction of the tabernacle, Moses would go there to meet with God to get his direction for the Israelites. During David's time, the tabernacle was still God's dwelling place and the Israelites would even take the Ark to battle with them because they understood that they needed God's presence.

In today's society, Christians are God's dwelling place. God, in the person of the Holy Spirit, lives within us as His tabernacle. Therefore, the question David asks is even more interesting because it impacts each Christian and our lifestyle.

David answers the question with a series of statements to identify the character of those who may dwell in God's presence. Notice the first statement says, "He who walks with integrity [blameless];" the second statement says, "He who works righteousness;" and the third statement says "He who speaks the truth in his heart." The concepts are in our walk [blameless character], our work [righteous conduct], and our speech [truthful conversation]. It's interesting to note that these three words are present participles, which means we are constantly obeying God and seeking to please Him. When you consider how the Lord is described in Scripture, these three concepts should cause us to carefully examine ourselves. The Lord is blameless in who He is (1 John 1:5-7), righteous in what He does (Ezra 9:15), and truthful in what He says (1 Samuel 15:29), and He wants His guests in the tabernacle to have the same characteristics.

To amplify these three concepts and make more specific applications, let's look more closely at them. When we consider that God dwells in us, it should make us more aware of our need to live in integrity and use these character statements to guide our lives.

The Oxford English Dictionary states that the word "integrity" comes from the Latin "integritas" which means "wholeness," "entireness," and "completeness." The root word is "integer" which means "untouched," "intact," "entire." Wiersbe (1988) states, "A person with integrity is not divided (that's duplicity) or merely pretending (that's hypocrisy). He or she is 'whole'; life is 'put together,' and things are working together harmoniously. People with integrity have nothing to hide and nothing to fear" (p. 21).

Matthew 6:19-24 describes integrity according to Jesus:

Do not lay up for yourselves treasures on earth, where moth and rust destroy and where thieves break in and steal; but lay up for yourselves treasures in heaven, where neither moth nor rust destroys and where thieves do not break in and steal. For where your treasure is, there your heart will be also.

The lamp of the body is the eye. If therefore your eye is good, your whole body will be full of light. But if your eye is bad, your whole body will be full of darkness. If therefore the light that is in you is darkness, how great is that darkness!

No one can serve two masters; for either he will hate the one and love the other, or else he will be loyal to the one and despise the other. You cannot serve God and mammon.

Consider the thoughts in this passage. A person with integrity will have a single heart. He doesn't try to love God and the world at the same time. He also will have a single mind which keeps him going in the right direction. After all, James 1:8 tells us that a "double minded man in unstable in all his ways." A man with integrity will also have a single will; he will seek to serve only one master. No one can be successful serving two masters at the same time (Wiersbe, 1988).

Chapter 6

Understanding Your Ministry

I believe another important area to consider for Christian educators is in regard to our ministry to our students and their families. We have discussed the spiritual aspects of our personal lives, but how does that translate into the ministry to which God has called us? Once again, if you teach in a Christian school, this outreach will be easier to accomplish. However, if you are in a secular school, don't forget about your responsibility as a Christian to be a witness to those around you. Take advantage of the opportunities that do arise and ask God to clearly show you those opportunities when they show up.

Students in a Christian school should be under the conviction of God's Word because our Christian educators teach the Word and live the Word. In that kind of an environment, a student may resist for a period of time, but the Holy Spirit will take everything we say and everything we do (as long as it is based on the Word of God) and use it for conviction. Our problem, however, is that many times we don't teach the Word and live the Word in a way that shows our genuine love and passion for God. Why should students desire something that doesn't seem to be real in their teachers' lives? We must remember though that some students will resist the conviction and not accept

Christ. We have no control over that other than we should continue being faithful in teaching the Word and living the Word.

We had a student in our Christian school several years ago that was not a Christian and would tell you that he was not, although he was not belligerent about it. We prayed continually for him and at the end of his senior year we thought we had failed in reaching his heart with the Gospel. He went away to college and several years later he showed up in our church one Sunday morning. As I was able to talk to him, he shared with me that he had recently accepted Christ as his Savior. He stated that all of the times he had heard the Gospel while in school finally caught up with him and he gave his life to Christ. He said it was the message he heard from teachers who had shown him that they cared about him. What a joy to know that even when we think we haven't been successful, God can still take the lessons we have taught and use them for His purpose.

As we reach the students, we also have the opportunity to minister to their parents. Do we make it a point to talk to the parents about God? When we have parent meetings, do we focus on the spiritual aspects of what we are discussing, or do we only focus on academic or behavior issues? When we deal with discipline issues, do we approach the issues from a Biblical perspective? Too often we don't even think about the opportunities God gives us to share the truths of His Word. Once again, this should be a natural part of our lives because of our passion for God and because of living a life committed to Christ.

I was speaking to the father of two of our students one day about the impact of our Biblical teaching on him and his wife. He told me that his wife was not saved, but talked about how she was memorizing verses with her children and singing the Christian songs that we were teaching the students in our school. His comment was,

"You don't have any idea what an impact you are making, in an indirect way, in my wife's life from a spiritual perspective."

I would like to insert some thoughts here that are directed specifically to Christian school educators. I believe that over the years, many of our Christian schools have lost their major focus of evangelizing and/or discipling the students. We have been sucked into the norms of our society and have placed the priorities of our schools on academics, athletics, fine arts, etc. instead of keeping the priority on spiritual things. Please understand, I believe all of these things are important, but when they are placed above our primary goal, we have problems. I believe a Christian school should be a school of excellence in everything we do and should have a strong academic program. My wife would tell you that I have spent much of my life taking classes, earning degrees, and attending seminars because I do consider academics to be important. I believe Christian school students should have the opportunities to participate in excellent athletics and fine arts programs as a part of developing a well-balanced life, with which they can bring glory to God. The question I am raising is in regard to how much effort is placed in our academic classrooms, with our athletic teams or fine arts groups, or even our parent meetings in sharing the Gospel.

However, our main priority, along with providing a strong academic education, is to produce Christian students with a passion for Christ. Our goal is to do everything we do to bring glory to God. We all know of many students who attend Christian schools for years and never make a profession of faith in Christ. We know of other students who make a profession of faith but are not prepared spiritually for what they will face in the world that awaits them. We must keep our focus on Christ and train our students appropriately in God's truth.

Unfortunately, many Christian schools have become "agents of behavior modification." Our teaching has become focused on getting students to obey our rules and regulations. We think that as long as the students comply with our standards and talk the Christian vocabulary, we have reached them with the Gospel. Unfortunately, many students have learned how to "play the game" and get by without anyone really confronting them with the truth of the Scripture. They comply to keep us happy and to keep us from "badgering" them with Christianity. We need to pray for our students on a regular basis for God to convict their heart in regard to their relationship with Christ. I know of a number of teachers who get to school early every day so they can pray for each student at the desk that student will be sitting in. Other teachers pray regularly for students as they enter their grades on the computer. Prayer does make a difference!

We know standards are necessary for organizations and especially schools, but our standards have nothing to do with being spiritual. We need to emphasize that many of our standards are put in place for organizational purposes, not for spiritual purposes. Every organization has some type of standards and schools are no different in that regard. Because of our focus on standards, we can inadvertently lead the students to conclude they can please God by living according to the standards. They think that just because they keep the rules, they are a Christian. They, and we, need to be reminded of Isaiah 29:13, *"Wherefore the Lord said, Forasmuch as this people draw near Me with their mouth, and with their lips do honor Me, but have removed their heart far from Me, and their fear toward Me is taught by the precept of men."*

We have mentioned several times about the importance of Christian educators being a proper example to the students. We must be careful that we don't fall into the same trap that some of our students fall into – the trap of living according to the rules rather than living for God. Isn't it amazing that students are so discerning sometimes about the spirituality of their teachers? We have a hard time convincing the students the importance of godliness if we don't exhibit it in our own lives.

Some think that teaching character is an answer. Character is good, as we have discussed earlier in this book. However, character can have an unbiblical motivation behind it. "True character is not learned; it is produced. It springs out of a mind that is so focused on the Lord that one changes into His image" (Hamrick, 2005, p. 16).

Hamrick (2005) summarizes his thoughts on this concept by stating, "Simply put, a God-focused ministry is one in which both the goal and the methods of ministry are designed to magnify the majesty of God so much that young people develop a passion for Him that governs every aspect of their lives" (p. 17).

May each of us be challenged to commit our lives to be holy before God and therefore, a proper example for our students and their parents.

Chapter 7

Building Proper Relationships

Building proper relationships is very important for any Christian, but especially for Christian educators. This chapter will focus on the various aspects of building proper relationships with various groups of people that will impact our ministry.

Kevin Myers and John Maxwell (2014) describe this concept very well in their book entitled, *Home Run*. They use the concept of a baseball diamond with each Christian starting at home plate as the batter. The only way we can get on base is to <u>connect</u> with Christ. At first base we build our <u>character</u> and at second base we build our <u>relationships</u>. Only then do we get to third base where we see results by developing <u>competence</u>. As we give God the glory for what we are able to accomplish, we are able to score and be ready for our next time at bat. Notice that character needs to be established before you can build relationships or you are running the bases out of order and you cannot be successful in those relationships.

Relationship with God

We have discussed this concept already, but I felt it should be mentioned again because of how important it is. As we build this relationship, we must spend time with the Lord in Bible study and prayer so we become better acquainted with Him. Eavey (1971) wrote,

> "First, last, and always, the truly Christian educator will realize his utter dependence upon the Spirit of God. The work that he is doing is God's work; he himself can never be other than a channel through which God operates. So the Christian educator can put his trust in the Holy Spirit to guide and to work through him, making him more and more nearly perfect in teaching God's truth to man" (p. 344).

Relationship to Bible and Prayer

I know this is not typically thought of as a relationship, but I believe it is important to have a proper relationship with these two sources of building our relationship with God. The Bible is our only textbook on living because it is through God's Word that we find God's will for our lives. A Christian educator should spend time in the Word of God each day and this will result in: (1) a desire for wisdom (James 1:5); (2) a surrendered body (Romans 12:1-2); (3) a trust for bearing fruit (John 15:16); (4) a request for power, love, and a sound mind (2 Timothy 1:7); (5) a trust in the Lord (Proverbs 3:5-7); and (6) death to self (John 12:24); as well as many other results.

Time spent in prayer is usually associated with the discipline of reading the Bible on a daily basis. Reading the Word is God speaking to us and prayer is our speaking to God. This communication builds our relationship. Too many times our prayers are totally focused on our wants and needs. Prayer should involve a time of confession, a time of thanksgiving, as well as a time of requesting. We should be praying for our administration, for our colleagues, for our students, for their families, as well as for God to work in our own lives to give us wisdom and discernment in our dealings with these various groups of people.

Relationship to the Local Church

There is much debate in regard to the place of the local church in the life of a Christian in general but in particular in regard to the life of a Christian educator teaching in a Christian school. It is important to understand that when we accepted Christ as our Savior, we became a part of the body of Christ, which many will refer to as the "Universal Church." However, it is difficult to have a proper "Christian" relationship with other Christians aside from the local church aspect because we cannot minister effectively to them using our spiritual gifts in a universal church; hence the importance of the local church. We must remember that Christ founded the church and He gave His life for the church. If Christ placed that much emphasis on the church, we must be faithful in our attendance, our ministry, and our support of the church of which we are a member.

Each Christian has been gifted with at least one spiritual gift at the time of salvation and the purpose of this gift is to equip us for a ministry to meet the needs of others. This ministry is typically done through the local church. If we are not faithful to a local church, we are not using our gifts as God intended and, therefore, are falling short of God's expectations of us.

For educators in a church-related Christian school, there is always discussion over whether the ministry of the educator in the school during the week can replace the ministry in the local church on weekends and mid-week. The Scripture teaches us that each Christian, as a member of a local church, has a ministry to fulfill based on the spiritual gifts God has given us. If you consider your ministry in the Christian school as fulfilling your Scriptural obligation for ministering in your church, I believe you are not placing the emphasis on the church that Christ did. You do use your giftedness outside of the local church to minister to the needs of others, but the purpose of that ministering is to draw people to Christ and to become a part of the local church.

Another issue is in regard to whether a church-related Christian school should require their school educators to attend the sponsoring church, or if they should be permitted to attend elsewhere. I am not going to deal with this issue because I believe it is the prerogative of the school and the sponsoring church to make that decision in regard to their employees. I don't believe it is a spiritual decision. However, I will state that if your Christian school requires you to attend the sponsoring church, then you should either do that faithfully or find another school in which to teach. To not attend is an act of rebellion, regardless of the reasons you may give.

If you teach in a secular school, it is also important for you to be faithful to your local church and to be involved in that ministry. This is one way that you will have an impact upon others in your school when conversation comes up regarding what you did on the weekend, etc. As you minister in your church and are involved in outreach events to the community, it is also a way for others to see that side of your life, and they will ask you questions about it. Be faithful and God will give you opportunities to be a testimony to those within your school.

Relationship to the School

The one word that comes to my mind when I consider a relationship with the school is loyalty. We must be loyal to the school and to the administration of the school. If you cannot be loyal for any reason, I believe it is time for you to move on to another school so you don't create division.

WANTED: Christian Educators with Character

To demonstrate that loyalty to the school you should be involved in as many activities as possible, without overloading yourself. God does not expect you to sacrifice your health or your family to be involved in activities. Depending on the size of the school, you may not be able to attend every activity, but at least attend and be involved in the major activities and as many others as possible.

You impact the students in your class when you attend their athletic events or fine arts events or other events. This is a part of building rapport with your students, which then helps you in building rapport with their parents because they see you showing an interest in their child.

If you never attend any activities, with the exception of the required ones, you are not showing your support of your school and it will weaken your relationship with the school and with others. Those teachers with young children must use discernment in this regard because your family does need to be a priority. However, there are some events that you can attend with your family, so don't use your family as an excuse for all events.

You also support your school by not getting involved in gossip or criticism about the school. If someone comes to you with criticism and you are not able to do anything to resolve the issue, you need to follow the Matthew 18 principle and take that person to the person who is able to deal with their criticism. Do not show agreement with the criticism. Likewise, if you have areas of concern about the school, you should take them to the appropriate administrator. Do not take your concerns to anyone who does not have control over that situation as it only causes division.

Relationship to the Administration

The Bible has much to say about our relationship with authority. Probably the most familiar passage is Romans 13. *"Let every soul be subject to the governing authorities. For there is no authority except from God, and the authorities that exist are appointed by God. Therefore whoever resists the authority resists the ordinance of God, and those who resist will bring judgment on themselves."* (vv. 1-2)

As we think about our relationship to the administration in our school, there are many thoughts that come to our minds. Some teachers are fortunate enough to have administrators who care about them and the students, and who are very involved in the educational process. Unfortunately, there are other teachers who deal with administrators who are rarely seen, and when they are seen, it is usually for something negative or more work that needs to be done.

However, Romans 13 doesn't specify our behavior in relationship to the type of authority we are under; our behavior is to be the same regardless because God has placed that authority over us for that specific time period. Ephesians 6:5-6 also gives us guidelines in regards to those who are in authority over us. Paul says *"be obedient to those who are your masters according to the flesh, with fear and trembling, in sincerity of heart, as to Christ; not with eyeservice, as men-pleasers, but as bondservants of Christ, doing the will of God from the heart."*

We must accept the admonition from the Scriptures as we seek to define our relationship with our administrators. If we don't submit to them, we are going against God's instruction for us and how then can we expect our students to submit to us?

We know there are times that our administrator must speak to us to correct us in areas in which we need to improve to be more effective. Even if the administrator approaches it the wrong way and says things that may seem harsh, we are to accept it and learn from it. We should accept it as a part of God's plan for making us a better teacher. We must have the mindset that God is using the administrators to equip us to be a more effective witness for Him.

We must learn to live within the organizational structure that exists in our school and we must be willing to work within the chain of command. To do otherwise is not Biblical. We may not agree with everything an administrator asks us to do. (When I was an administrator, I didn't always agree with everything I asked the teachers to do, but it was how it needed to be done to accomplish the goal of the ministry at that time.) When we disagree, we must not spread our disagreement to other teachers, our students, or the school parents. If we feel it is important, we should follow the Matthew 18 principle and go to the administrator to discuss it with them. If we still can't agree, we must make a decision that we will obey what we are asked to do, or we ultimately need to resign our position, because without unity we cannot achieve our goal as a school.

Relationship to our Colleagues

Paul stresses the concept of unity in his letter to the Ephesians. He states that unity is necessary for the body of Christ to function as it should. I recognize that those who teach in a secular school don't have the opportunity to experience this unity since they may be the only Christian on the faculty, or one of a small group of Christians. However, even in that situation, you should strive to be as unified as possible for the sake of the students, even though you will differ in your worldview.

Those who teach in a Christian school have a real advantage in this aspect because we are united in Christ, we have a similar worldview, and we are all serving Christ as we minister to the students. However, even in this situation, there will be difficult times when you don't get along with some of your colleagues. This is when you have to allow Christ to work in you and through you to maintain your testimony and the testimony of Christ. I was once told that if you have a disagreement with someone, pray for them. If you are praying for God's best for a person, it is difficult to not be in agreement with them.

There are several things that seem to cause division between teachers. One is when a teacher doesn't follow the same procedures as everyone else and the students use this against those who are following the correct procedures. You are to still do the right thing and it would be helpful for you to talk to the other teacher to explain how it is creating problems with the students. Likewise, students will sometimes go to a teacher and complain about another teacher. You have to be careful not to agree with them because that causes division. You should encourage the student to go and talk to the other teacher or offer to go with them to the other teacher. You must be careful about making any judgments against another teacher.

Once again, we have to be careful to follow the Matthew 18 principle of going to the one whom we have an issue with and discuss the situation to work it out between us.

Several ways we should develop and maintain a proper relationship with our colleagues would be to exercise kindness, encouragement, discretion, care, etc. In other words exhibit the fruit of the Spirit that we discussed in an earlier chapter.

Relationship to our Students

As we consider our relationship to our students, the topic is almost overwhelming to think about. We must build relationships with them, but we must be careful not to become too close to them, so we must find that proper balance in our relationship.

We cannot become their close friend. This can especially be a problem in the high school where a young teacher just out of college is teaching students who are only a few years younger. Teachers, as do all people, have a natural desire to be liked and sometimes will become too close to the students in an effort to build this relationship. The danger of becoming a friend shows up in the loss of respect on the part of the student. They begin to think that they can get by with doing things that other students can't because the teacher is his/her friend.

Another danger is the close relationships between a teacher and a student of the opposite gender. Teachers must not allow themselves to be taken in by a student who wants to spend time with them or to share their personal problems with them. A proper distance needs to be maintained so there is never any room to question the relationship. In our society today, people are very quick to judge and always think the worst is happening, even when it might not be. Never allow yourself to be alone with a student of the opposite gender, except in very public places. In today's society, we must also be careful with our relationship with students of the same gender.

We must care about our students and support our students as we work to meet their needs, but we must always maintain the professional teacher-student relationship with them. A Christian teacher needs to be available for a student who needs to talk, but must be wise as to the extent of this relationship without involving another person.

Relationship with Parents

How a teacher relates to the parents of the students he/she teaches can often get complicated because of such diverse situations that might be involved. I believe the first thing we need to remember and always keep as a priority is the Biblical principle that God has given the responsibility of raising their children to the parents, not the school or the educators. When students are enrolled in our school, we are there to assist the parents in the aspect of their education. We serve "in loco parentis" or in place of the parents during the hours we have them in our care. I have often had parents tell me that it seems that the teachers have more time with their children than they, as parents, have. This can be true, but it doesn't change the God-given responsibility to the parents.

This relationship with parents is another area that is very different between Christian schools and other private schools on one hand and charter schools and public schools on the other hand. This difference is the fact that in private schools, parents pay tuition for their children to be educated. When you are paying for an education for your child, you tend to be more involved and have higher expectations because you don't want to be wasting your money.

Some parents who pay tuition think that gives them the right to have a say in how the school is run and how their child is treated. This is why the school and the educators must make it very clear that if a parent enrolls their child in a private school, they must understand that they are agreeing with how the school is being operated and with the philosophy of the school. If they do not agree with this and want to see the school run differently, they need to withdraw their child and send them to a school where they can be in agreement. This is not to say that parents cannot make suggestions that they believe will make the school a better place. We should always listen to their suggestions, but we should never feel obligated to make changes just because of a parent's complaint.

From an educator's perspective, if a parent is paying for their child to get an education, we must be committed to providing the best education possible. All areas of the school's program must be geared toward excellence. As a Christian, we should want everything done to the best of our capability. If we cannot offer a quality program and if we can't teach the students the academics they need to be successful in life, we are cheating the parents and that impacts our relationship with them.

From the perspective of schools that don't charge tuition – charter and public – educators must still be careful with their relationships with parents from the standpoint of making sure the students are getting the best education possible. We may not be cheating them financially, as we would in a private school, but we are still cheating the students from being able to achieve their full potential in life.

Educators must keep the parents informed of how their child is doing in school. (Remember, parents have the God-given responsibility of raising their child and we are only there to help.) This may be done by various means of communication, with the most common means used today being emails and text messages. However, sometimes there needs to be more verbalization and discussion which can best be accomplished via a phone call. For other instances there needs to be a face-to-face meeting with everyone involved so non-verbal reactions are noted as well as verbal. Sometimes these meetings can accomplish a whole lot more than continuous emails going back and forth.

Communication is necessary to clarify various situations, especially when students say things at home or at school that can be misunderstood. Many agreements have been made between educators and parents to the effect that the educator won't believe everything the students tells them about what happened at home and the parents won't believe everything the student tells them about what happened at school. If there is a question, we must communicate! Don't try to hide anything from the parents. We must be honest with them. If you have a question as to whether you need to communicate with a parent, you need to ask yourself if you would want to know about it if it was your child. This is a good guideline, but always err toward too much communication as opposed to too little communication.

In church-sponsored Christian schools we have another dynamic of which we must be careful. This is the dynamic of going to the same church and worshiping together with a parent and an educator sitting side by side. This is not bad in itself, but once again, we must maintain a professional relationship in regard to school issues. I have taught children of good friends and have been in their homes for a meal and have ministered alongside of them in the church. For the most part, this can work as long as we are careful. However, there are times when the friendship is affected because of issues the child has in school. I have known many families who have left the church because of problems in the school with their child. The key is finding the balance between "school" and "out of school" areas of life. It can work but we must be cautious.

I would encourage every educator to attend school activities and mingle with the parents who are at that event. Over the years I have been able to develop some good friendships by talking to parents at the athletic events or the fine arts productions. The fact that you attend these activities and talk to the parents while you are there will be a great asset to you being able to witness to them over a period of time. Build those relationships with the parents in as many ways as possible.

Relationship with the Community

A Christian's relationship with the community can differ significantly depending on the type of school in which you teach. An educator in a public school within a community needs to develop a good relationship with those in the particular geographic area in which their school is located. However, an educator in a charter school or a private school typically serves a broader community, and not all of the families in the closer community. Nevertheless, it is important for all to develop and maintain a good relationship with those in the community.

Probably the most important aspect for a Christian educator is to "let their light shine" (Matthew 5:16) in such a way that their testimony is known in the community. People in the community should not have to wonder if a Christian educator has the proper character in their life. One of the most damaging aspects to a person's testimony is when they are not honest in their business dealings. It is important to pay your bills on time and to not expect any special considerations. It is important that you treat those you do business with in a respectful manner. For example, if you get upset about something with your bank and you yell at the bank teller or one of the bank officers, you will have a difficult time restoring that relationship and being able to ever be a testimony for Christ to them. I would encourage you to demonstrate your character and your Christian testimony in your dealings with those in the community.

As an example, my wife and I went into a fast food restaurant one day and there was a man standing at the counter who was visibly upset with the employee. I didn't pay a lot of attention to him or to what he was saying but after a few minutes he turned and saw me. He immediately changed his tone of voice and told the employee that it was okay and not to worry about the problem. He happened to be one of the parents (and a Christian) at the school of which I was principal at that time. Why did he change his behavior? Because he knew that a Christian shouldn't act like that and he needed to be more careful with his conversations. Please don't ever get caught in that kind of a situation!

Another aspect a Christian educator should consider is their involvement in the community and in community projects. If those in the community see you involved, they will have more respect for you and you will therefore be able to be a witness to them. I understand that sometimes we get so busy within our school and our other obligations it is difficult to find the time to get too involved in other projects. However, if you only pick one or two projects a year and commit a day or two to each one, you will broaden your impact.

As I close this chapter on building proper relationships, I would like to remind you that you are better able to have a witness to those you build proper relationships with. We must remember that our purpose as a Christian is to do everything to the glory of God and to be a witness to those to whom we come into contact. Sometimes we must not say what we are thinking and we must be careful with how we say things in order to not destroy our relationships.

Chapter 8

CONCLUSION

As I come to the conclusion of this book, I want to stress that this book has not been about the academic life of a Christian educator, but the personal life and somewhat about the professional life. I do believe it is essential that every Christian educator should strive to be the best educator they can be. Regardless of what type of school you teach in, you should provide the best academic education possible along with an education that is focused on Scripture or on Biblical principles. Every Christian educator should be involved in furthering their education and participating in professional development to learn how to be more effective in teaching their students. We should not be satisfied to stay on the academic level we are on currently. I believe that every Christian should be a reader and should keep up with the current trends in education.

Likewise, we should not be satisfied to remain on our current level in our spiritual life. That is why I consider the discussion of character to be so important. We have seen our society slide down the slope of mediocrity and some people settle for less than their best. This should not be true of Christians. I have heard many Christians, particularly those in public schools, say that teaching isn't worth the time and effort they must put in anymore. They express their feelings that they will continue to teach but will not put forth any more energy than what is required to get by. If we do this, we are insulting God because He gave His only Son for us – He gave us His best. I believe that Christians should feel called to their vocation and should see their vocation as their ministry. If you are called to be an educator, you must minister to those God has given you in the most effective way possible and must do your best in your teaching. We must see our students as a gift from God to whom we are privileged to minister. We all know there are difficult students in our classrooms. However, we must see them as God sees them and do our best to show them God's love through our teaching and our lives.

As Christians, we understand that all truth is God's truth. Because of this, we must recognize that education must "stand for and honor the truth wherever it is found" (Gaebelein, 1968, p. 23). Therefore, it is incumbent on all Christians to present the truth of God in whatever subject they teach. We must be careful with the curriculum that is being used in our school and determine if it agrees with God's truth. If it doesn't, we need to integrate Biblical principles in such a way that we are teaching truth and not just teaching the thoughts of men. Of course, this is easier to do in a Christian school than in a secular school and it is also easier if you are able to use a curriculum developed by Christians. However, this does not excuse others from taking a shortcut and not making sure they are teaching the truth. For example, to teach history that has no mention of the historical Christ is not a complete education and to teach science without at least discussing creationism is not total science.

I stated at the beginning of this book that one of the purposes in my writing is to help us understand who and what a Christian educator should be, based on Biblical principles. I don't believe we can really understand this without being challenged in our thinking, which was also a purpose of the book. It's not easy to live a totally committed

Christian life in our society today or in our schools today, but we must make every effort to do so. If you have been challenged, my goal has been partially fulfilled; if you have been challenged and as a result have been changed, my goal has been further fulfilled. May we continue to grow in Christ. As we build our relationship with Him, it is easier to build our relationship with others and to live a life of Biblical character.

In conclusion, consider the following from Philippians 3:7-11: *But what things were gain to me, these I have counted loss for Christ. Yet indeed I also count all things loss for the excellence of the knowledge of Christ Jesus my Lord, for whom I have suffered the loss of all things, and count them as rubbish, that I may gain Christ and be found in Him, not having my own righteousness, which is from the law, but that which is through faith in Christ, the righteousness which is from God by faith;* **_that I may know Him_** *and the power of His resurrection, and the fellowship of His sufferings, being conformed to His death, if, by any means, I may attain to the resurrection from the dead.*

REFERENCES

Bridges, J. (1996). *The pursuit of holiness*. Colorado Springs: NavPress.

Briscoe, S. (1993). *The fruit of the Spirit: Cultivating Christian character*. Wheaton, IL: Harold Shaw.

Colson, C. & Pearcey, N. (1999). *How now shall we live?* Wheaton, IL: Tyndale House.

Covey, S.R. (1989). *The 7 habits of highly effective people*. New York: Simon & Schuster.

Eavey, C.B. (1971). *Principles of teaching for Christian educators*. Grand Rapids, MI: Zondervan.

Gaebelein, F. E. (1968). *The pattern of God's truth*. Chicago: Moody Press.

Gateway to Better Education. (www.gtbe.org)

Getz, G.A. (1974). *The measure of a man*. Ventura, CA: Regal Books.

Greear, J.D. (2011). *Gospel*. Nashville, TN: B & H Books.

Hamrick, F. (2005). *The heart of the matter: The God-focused school*. Whitakers, NC: Positive Action for Christ.

Hybels, B. (1987). *Who you are when no one's looking*. Downers Grove, IL: InterVarsity.

Jacquot, A. (1984). Guide to successful Christian teaching. Fairfax, VA: American Association of Christian Schools.

Johnson, P.E. (2002). *The right questions: Truth, meaning, & public debate*. Downers Grove, IL: InterVarsity.

Lloyd-Jones, D.M. (1976). *Studies in the sermon on the mount*. Grand Rapids, MI: Eerdmans.

Lowrie, R.W. (1978). *To those who teach in Christian schools*. Colorado Springs, CO: ACSI.

Myers, K. & Maxwell, J.C. (2014). *Home run.* New York: FaithWords.

Pearcey, N.R. (2005). *Total truth: Liberating Christianity from its cultural captivity.* Wheaton, IL: Crossway.

Stanley, A. (1997). *Like a rock: Becoming a person of character.* Nashville: Thomas Nelson.

Swindoll, C.R. (1981). *Improving your serve.* Waco, TX: Word.

Van Brummelen, H. (2009). *Walking with God in the classroom.* Colorado Springs, CO: Purposeful Design.

White, J. (1979). *Honesty, morality, & conscience.* Colorado Springs: NavPress.

Wiersbe, W.W. (1988). *The integrity crisis.* Nashville: Thomas Nelson.

ABOUT THE AUTHOR

Dr. Jim Virtue has served for over 45 years in both Christian educational and pastoral ministries. He attended Baptist Bible College and graduated from Evangel College with his BS degree in Religion and Philosophy. He continued his education at Florida International University where he earned his MS and EdD in Educational Administration and Supervision. He also earned his MAR from Liberty University.

Dr. Virtue began his educational career at Dade Christian School in Miami, FL, teaching math, science, and Bible on a high school level and after ten years in various positions, became the Head of School. After 13 years in that position, he resigned and served on the pastoral staff of the sponsoring church for six years. The church started another school, The Master's Academy, and he assumed the position of principal there and served for ten years. He also served as Superintendent over both schools and as the Discipleship Pastor prior to retiring.

Following retirement, Dr. Virtue has served in several schools as an Interim Headmaster, a Director of Staff Development, and as a consultant. He serves as an Adjunct Professor in the School of Education for Liberty University Online and also teaches Bible classes periodically at Trinity International University – South Florida Campus.